Name: _____

Class: _____

Teacher: _____

Islamic Studies Textbook Level 4

Minhaj-ul-Quran International

Published by

Minhaj-ul-Quran Publications
30 Brindley Road
Manchester
M16 9HQ (UK)

Acknowledgements

Bilal Hussain, Safina Nazir, Muhammad Zeeshan Qadri, Ali Akbar, Raffiq Patel and M. Dawood Mehmood

A sincere thank you to Ajmal Khan for his assistance in the design work

ISBN: 978-1-908229-58-8

www.minhajpublications.com

www.islamforkids.org.uk

First published August 2018

Printed by Elma Printing in Turkey

Islamic Studies
Textbook Level 4

Series Editors

Waqas Ahmed Amin

Jawed Iqbal Tahiri

Mariam Khalid

Series Director

Tahseen Khalid

Minhaj-ul-Quran International

Preface

In the name of Allah, the Most Merciful, the Most Kind.

WE PRAISE ALLAH that the Muslim community has come a long way since the days when the first immigrants settled in Britain. From that time till today, there have been significant developments in the quality of educational material being produced by British Muslims. Many advancements have been made in this regard such that English is fast becoming one of the academic languages of Islam, alongside Arabic, Persian, Urdu and Turkish.

The importance of education cannot be overstated. The British Muslim community has put great effort into imparting Islamic knowledge to their children. Islamic classes and religious seminaries have been established up and down the country for the single goal of teaching the coming generations the fundamentals of their religion. Among those that have been at the forefront in this regard is Minhaj-ul-Quran International, a global organisation with branches in over 90 countries.

As an organisation, Minhaj-ul-Quran International seeks to uplift Muslims worldwide through the revival of education and spirituality. It established its first branch in the United Kingdom in the late 1980s and founded its first centre in the 1990s. For more than two decades it has endeavoured to provide for the educational and spiritual needs of the Muslim diaspora of Great Britain.

The 'Islam for Kids' initiative is part of the longstanding services of Minhaj-ul-Quran International. This Islamic Studies series was produced and developed by second and third generation British scholars, who are trained classically in the traditional Islamic sciences, alongside QTS (Qualified Teaching Status) accredited teachers. It is an indigenous and local endeavour by the UK branch of Minhaj-ul-Quran International to fulfil the educational needs of native English-speaking students.

The Syllabus

The 'Islam for Kids' Islamic Studies series has been split into six levels with each level corresponding to the years of the state-funded education system in the UK. It is recommended to start level one at the age of 5 when the child starts year one at primary school and to complete level 6 by the age of 11 when the child completes his or her primary school education. However, the series can be started earlier at an earlier age or later depending on the ability of the student.

The six levels have been grouped into three stages, with each stage consisting of two levels. In the first stage, which consists of levels one and two, the aim is to ease the child into understanding Islamic concepts and terminology. The purpose of this stage is not to burden the child with technical knowledge about Islam, but rather to simply instil in them a sense of Muslim identity and to explore key Islamic concepts.

Traditionally, Muslim parents have been advised to have a play-based approach with their children's learning for the first seven years and then to formally teach them for the next seven years. Following this advice, in the first two years of the syllabus, a more visual approach has been adopted with the text being kept at a minimum. This enables the content to be taught in a child-friendly manner and allows teachers and parents to make the lessons more interactive and engaging for the child.

The second stage of the syllabus begins at level three when the child reaches seven years of age. From this level onwards, a more formal approach to learning is adopted. Many of the concepts in the first stage are revisited, but instead of being largely pictorial, they are more text-based so that the key concepts can be conveyed in detail to the child and to encourage the child to start thinking about the content in more depth.

In the third stage of the syllabus, which consists of levels five and six, the series shifts to a more text-heavy approach. This is to encourage the child to learn independently and practice their key reading and comprehension skills. The content at this level increases in difficulty to engage students academically and to raise the standard of literacy and understanding of Islamic concepts.

The concepts from the previous two stages are revisited in this third stage but in much more detail. Parents and teachers alike will find this stage beneficial as reading material to help prepare in terms of subject knowledge for teaching the lessons in the earlier two stages. In this way, the three stages work together to ease the child into becoming well acquainted with Islamic terminology, concepts and values.

By the end of this syllabus, the child will have acquired the essential Islamic knowledge (*Fard `Ayn*) for them to be able to live their life as a practising Muslim. This Islamic Studies series is an excellent resource for parents to lay the foundation for their child's learning. If Allah wills, further levels will be added to this syllabus, thus enhancing the child's understanding of Islam and enabling them to become lifelong learners of the Islamic tradition.

The First Edition

In preparation of this series, authentic and reliable content was taken from the works of great scholars who represent Islamic orthodoxy. Some of the books that were consulted in the creation of the content were:

- Imam ash-Shurunbulali's *Nur al-Idah* and its commentary, *Maraqi al-Falah*
- Imam al-Laqqani's *Jawharah at-Tawhid*
- Shaykh Salih Farfur's *ar-Risalah an-Nafi`ah fi `Ilm at-Tawhid*
- Imam Ibn Hisham's *as-Sirah an-Nabawiyyah* (including its English rendition by Martin Lings)
- Imam Ibn Kathir's *al-Bidayah wa an-Nihayah*
- and the many hadith collections compiled by the founder of Minhaj-ul-Quran, Shaykh-ul-Islam Dr Muhammad Tahir-ul-Qadri

The contents of these books have been adapted for children at an age appropriate level while keeping in consideration the specific needs and requirements of Western Muslims.

We are eager to hear from the wider community and to gain feedback regarding the series. For this purpose, we have set up an email address for you to send us your feedback. You can contact us at the following address: feedback@fmriuk.org.

Acknowledgements

Before closing, I would like to thank my co-editors, Jawed Iqbal Tahiri and Mariam Khalid, for their commitment and assistance in helping to prepare and develop the contents of this syllabus. I would also like to thank the Series Director, Tahseen Khalid, for his great determination and support in bringing this series to fruition.

I would also like to thank Bilal Hussain, for his assistance in preparing the outline of the syllabus, and the Textbook Review Team (Safina Nazir, Muhammad Zeeshan Qadri, Ali Akbar, Raffiq Patel and Dawood Mehmood) for their feedback and support. A special thank you goes to Ajmal Khan for the outstanding devotion he has shown in improving and further developing the design work.

I pray to Allah that He accepts our efforts and makes it a means of salvation for us in this life and the next, and we pray that this series becomes a means of uplifting the Ummah for generations to come.

Amin bi-jahi Sayyid al-Mursalin ﷺ

Waqas Ahmed Amin
Minhaj-ul-Quran Publications
1st Dhu al-Hijjah 1439 AH/12th August 2018 CE

Contents

Lesson 1

The Articles of Faith

To believe in something is called '**faith**'. The Arabic term for faith is '**Iman**'. As a Muslim, we must believe in seven important things. These seven things are known as the '**Articles of Faith**'. If someone does not believe in any of the Articles of Faith, he or she cannot be a Muslim.

The Articles of Faith have been mentioned several times in the Qur'an and the hadith of Prophet Muhammad ﷺ. For example, in the Qur'an Allah says: "*He who disbelieves in Allah, His angels, His Books, His Messengers and the Last Day has surely gone far away (from the truth).*" (an-Nisa' 4:136)

In the hadith, they have been mentioned in the '**Hadith Jibra'il**', in which it is reported that Angel Jibra'il ﷺ came in the form of a man to ask the Prophet ﷺ several questions. One of the questions were: "What is Iman (faith)?" And the Prophet ﷺ replied, "Iman (faith) is to believe in Allah, His angels, His Books, His Messengers, the Last Day and to believe in the Divine Decree – both its good and bad."

The 'Articles of Faith' can be found in the following statement known as '**al-Iman al-Mufassal**' (The Detailed Beliefs).

Al-Iman al-Mufassal

آمَنْتُ بِاللهِ وَمَلَائِكَتِهِ وَكُتُبِهِ وَرُسُلِهِ
وَالْيَوْمِ الْآخِرِ وَالْقَدْرِ خَيْرِهِ وَشَرِّهِ مِنَ اللهِ تَعَالَى
وَالْبَعْثِ بَعْدَ الْمَوْتِ.

I believe in Allah, His angels, His Books,
His Messengers, the Last Day,
the Divine Decree — that good and bad
comes from Allah — and life after death.

The seven Articles of Faith are mentioned in detail below.

1. Belief in Allah

We believe in Allah. He is the One and Only God and the Maker of everything. We do not worship anyone but Him.

2. Belief in the Angels

We believe in the angels. Angels are Allah's special servants who are given specific duties by Allah. They are made from light and they do not disobey Allah.

3. Belief in the Holy Books

We believe in the original Holy Books that were revealed by Allah to past Prophets and Messengers for our guidance.

4. Belief in the Prophets and Messengers

We believe in all the Prophets and Messengers who were sent by Allah. They taught people the message of Allah and told them what is right and what is wrong.

5. Belief in the Last Day

We believe in the Last Day when Allah will judge us. All our actions will be weighed to see whether we have been good or bad. Those whose good deeds are heavier will go to Paradise and those whose bad deeds are heavier will go to the Hellfire.

6. Belief in the Divine Decree

We believe that everything good and bad is from Allah. Allah is the One Who controls everything, and nothing takes place except by His power and will.

7. Belief in Life after Death

We believe that after death, we will be questioned in the grave about our religion and be rewarded or punished. Then on the Day of Judgement, we will be brought back to life again to answer Allah for all our actions in this life.

Lesson 2

Belief in Allah

We believe in Allah. Allah is the Arabic word for God.

As a Muslim, we believe that there is NO god but Allah. Allah is One and we do not worship anyone or anything besides Him.

Allah has no partner, and nothing is equal to Him. He made everything, and nothing is like Him.

Allah has no father or mother. Allah gave us parents to look after us, but Allah does not need anyone to look after Him. Allah does not need a mother or father.

Allah has no son or daughter. No one can be Allah's son or daughter because no one is like Allah. If Allah had a son or daughter, then he or she would be like Him, but no one is like Allah. So how can Allah have a son or a daughter?

Allah is not a person and He does not have a body. People have bodies. We have two eyes, two ears, a mouth and a nose. Allah made these for us because we are people and we need a body. Allah is the Maker. He is the One Who makes people and their bodies; He does not need a body.

There is nothing like Allah. No one looks like Allah, and Allah does not look like anyone or anything else. Allah has made us either a boy or a girl. But Allah is not a boy or a girl, nor a man or woman. He is so great that we cannot imagine Him.

Whatever we believe about Allah must be according to the teachings of Prophet Muhammad ﷺ. The Prophet ﷺ taught us about **Allah**, **His Names** and **Attributes**. And we must believe in everything the Prophet ﷺ taught us about Him.

Our belief in Allah can be found in the following statement known as '**al-Iman al-Mujmal**' (The General Beliefs).

Al-Iman al-Mujmal

آمَنْتُ بِاللهِ كَمَا هُوَ بِأَسْمَائِهِ وَصِفَاتِهِ وَقَبِلْتُ جَمِيْعَ أَحْكَامِهِ إِقْرَاراً بِاللِّسَانِ وَتَصْدِيْقاً بِالْقَلْبِ.

I believe in Allah as He is with His Names and Attributes, and I accept all His Commands affirming them with the tongue and believing in them with the heart.

From this statement, we must know the following things:

We Must Believe in Allah as He is

- We must believe about Allah only what Prophet Muhammad ﷺ taught us. This means that we must believe in Allah as He is described in the Qur'an and hadith.

- We should never make things up about Allah. Our minds cannot understand Allah's nature. Allah is beyond our imaginations and thoughts. Whatever comes to our mind, Allah is greater than it.

We Believe in Him with His Names and Attributes

- We must believe in Allah's Names as they have come to us through the Qur'an and hadith. There are 99 Beautiful Names of Allah, which describe Allah's Being, Attributes and Actions.

- We must believe in Allah's Attributes, which are His characteristics. There are eight important characteristics that we must believe in. They are that Allah is existing, living, knowledgeable, willing, powerful, seeing, hearing and speaking.

Lesson 3

Prophet `Isa ﷺ – Birth and Childhood

Lady Maryam was a very good and pious young lady. She used to worship Allah all day and night. One day, the Angel Jibra'il ﷺ came to her in the form of a man. Lady Maryam was afraid; she told him that if he feared Allah then he would stay away from her. But the Angel told her not to be afraid of him because he was a messenger from Allah sent to grant Lady Maryam a pious son, whose name will be `Isa.

Lady Maryam was surprised by what Angel Jibra'il ﷺ told her. She told Angel Jibra'il that she could not have a child because she was not married. But Angel Jibra'il ﷺ assured her that it was Allah's command and Allah is most powerful over everything. Angel Jibra'il ﷺ then

blew on Lady Maryam, and he left. Lady Maryam accepted Allah's decision and she put her full trust in Allah, because she knew that Allah would never let anything bad happen to her.

When the time for the baby's birth approached, Lady Maryam went to a quiet place in the nearby town called Bethlehem. She sat near a date-palm tree because she was feeling a lot of pain. A voice called out to her telling her not to worry, because she could drink water from the small nearby river and she could shake the date-palm tree next to her and eat the dates. Allah ordered Lady Maryam not to speak to anyone, and to keep a vow of silence.

After the birth of Prophet `Isa ﷺ, Lady Maryam returned to her people with the newborn baby in her arms. When the people saw the baby, they were surprised and astonished. They started to question Lady Maryam and asked her who the baby's father was. They started saying that she did something very bad and teased her, saying, "Your father was not a bad man and your mother was not a bad woman." But Lady Maryam did not say anything.

She did not reply to the people, but she pointed to the newborn baby. The people said, "How can a newborn baby speak while being in the cradle?" As they said this, the newborn baby spoke and said, "I am the servant of Allah. He has given me the book and has made me a Prophet."

When the people heard the newborn speaking from the cradle, they were surprised and shocked. They saw this miracle and they knew that Maryam was truthful. Lady Maryam had trust in Allah and Allah helps those who trust Him.

The news of Prophet `Isa's birth spread far and wide. The Roman King who ruled over Palestine learned about this. The Bani Isra'il warned the King that one day Prophet `Isa عليه السلام will grow to become a leader, and he will bring an end to his rule. Hearing this, the King got worried and he ordered his soldiers to go to Jerusalem and find Prophet `Isa عليه السلام, and to kill him. Allah sent His angels to Lady Maryam to tell her about the King's plan. So, she decided to leave Jerusalem and take Prophet `Isa ﷺ with her to live in Egypt.

While Prophet `Isa ﷺ was growing up in Egypt, Allah gifted him with many miracles. He would tell the other children what their mothers cooked at home. When the children went back home, they would tell their mothers what was made, and their mothers would be surprised that they would know this. Prophet `Isa ﷺ would tell others what they stored in their houses and where they had hidden their money.

When Prophet `Isa ﷺ grew up to become a young man, he returned to Jerusalem. Allah gave him a holy book called the 'Injil' (the Gospel). He called the people to the worship of the One God, Allah. He taught the Bani Isra'il the commands of Allah. He taught people to be good and to respect their parents and to show kindness to the poor and the weak. But the Bani Isra'il did not listen to Prophet `Isa ﷺ; they were disobedient. They would say that `Isa ﷺ was not the Prophet of Allah.

Lesson 4

Prophet `Isa ﷺ – Miracles and Raising to the Heavens

Allah wanted the Bani Isra'il to be guided to the truth, so He gave Prophet `Isa ﷺ many signs, called miracles.

Among Prophet `Isa's miracles was that he would cure the sick and weak. He cured those who were born blind. He also cured the lepers (people who had skin diseases). In that time, no medicine or doctor could cure this illness, but Prophet `Isa ﷺ with Allah's help made them healthy again. He would also make birds out of clay and then breathe into them; the birds would come to life and they would fly away. He also brought dead people back to life by Allah's help.

All these miracles were to show the Bani Isra'il that he was the Prophet of Allah, so that they may be guided. The poor and the weak people from the Bani Isra'il listened to Prophet `Isa ﷺ and they followed his teachings, but the rich and powerful did not.

Prophet `Isa ﷺ chose some people to be his helpers, and they were known as the 'Hawariyyun' (disciples). They travelled with Prophet `Isa ﷺ and helped him to teach the people and to spread the message of the worship of the One God, Allah.

The Hawariyyun (disciples) asked Prophet `Isa ﷺ for a table of food from Heaven, so that they may eat from it and celebrate it as a day of `Id. Allah told the Hawariyyun (disciples) that He will send the table of food from Heaven, but whoever still did not believe in Allah after this, they would get punished with a punishment that had never been seen before.

The table of food came down from the sky and it contained seven types of fish, seven kinds of bread and different kinds of fruits. The followers of Prophet `Isa عليه السلام ate from the food and they enjoyed it. Everyone ate from it, the rich and the poor, and the strong and the weak. The sick people who ate from it got healed and they were no longer sick. The followers of Prophet `Isa عليه السلام received many blessings because of it.

Prophet `Isa عليه السلام saw that the Bani Isra'il would not obey Allah; the rich people lied, cheated and stole the money of the poor people. He told them not to disobey Allah and to be good, but they did not listen. Instead, they turned against him and they called on the Roman King to send his soldiers to kill him.

When the soldiers reached outside the house, Allah raised Prophet `Isa عليه السلام to the heavens. Allah then changed the face of one of the people from the Bani Isra'il to look like Prophet `Isa عليه السلام. The soldiers believed that this man was Prophet `Isa عليه السلام, so they arrested him. This man looked very much like Prophet `Isa عليه السلام, but he was not him. The soldiers took this man and they brought him in front of the people. They placed this man on a big cross and they killed him.

The followers of Prophet `Isa ﷺ were very confused about this. They did not know that Allah raised him to the Heavens. Only a small number of people knew the truth. The followers of Prophet `Isa ﷺ started disagreeing with one another about this. Some people started calling Prophet `Isa ﷺ God and others said that he was God's son!

Prophet Muhammad ﷺ taught us the truth that `Isa ﷺ was a Prophet and Servant of Allah. He did not die on the cross, but he is still alive in the Heavens, and before the Last Day he will return to the earth again. When Prophet `Isa ﷺ will return, he will tell people the truth and he will call everyone to the worship of the One God.

Lesson 5

Allah is Forever

Allah is forever. This means that Allah has no beginning and no end. Allah was not born, and He will not die.

Everything besides Allah has a beginning and an end.

The sun, moon and stars were made by Allah a very long time ago, and so they have a beginning; and one day, a long time in the future, they will come to an end.

The mountains, skies and seas were all made by Allah. They all have a beginning, and before the Last Day, they will also come to an end.

Allah made the animals, birds and fishes. There was a day when they were born; and when they die, they will also come to an end.

Even we are born into this world, and one day we will die also, when Allah decides. This shows us that we too have a beginning and an end.

Every human being is a creation of Allah. They were made by Him. No human being can make himself. His life

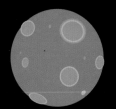

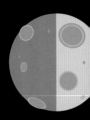

is given to him by Allah, the All-Powerful Creator.

Only the Creator, the One Who made us all, can be the One True God. If someone is born and is a baby in the cradle, it means he cannot be God, but only a creation of Allah.

This is because a person who is born or dies cannot control his own life, and so that person cannot be God.

Everything we see, hear or touch is Allah's creation. Allah made everything, and no one made Allah. There is nothing in the whole universe that is not Allah's creation.

Allah has always been 'the Maker' and 'the Creator'. Even when there was nothing, Allah was alive. Allah said, 'Be', and He made the whole universe from nothing.

When we were born, we were small, and every day we grew bigger until we could walk and talk. We kept on changing, but Allah does not change.

Allah was never small, and He does not grow. He is the same today just like He was in the past and will continue to be the same in the future just like He is today. This is because Allah does not change, and He is forever.

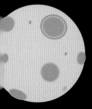

Lesson 6

Respecting Parents

Respecting, being kind to and looking after parents is very important in Islam. Allah shows us how important it is by mentioning this in the Qur'an right next to the command that tells us to worship Him.

In the Qur'an, Allah says: "*And your Lord has commanded you not to worship anyone other than Allah and treat parents with kindness. If either or both of them attain old age, then do not say even 'Ugh!' to them, nor blame them. And always speak to both of them humbly, observing polite manners.*" (Bani Isra'il 17:23)

Once a man asked Prophet Muhammad ﷺ, "What is the responsibility children have towards their parents?" The Prophet ﷺ replied, "They are your Paradise and your Hell." This means that if you treat your parents well then you will go to Paradise and if you disobey them and treat them badly then you will deserve to go to Hell.

`Abd Allah bin Mas`ud asked the Prophet ﷺ, "Which action does Allah love the most?" The Prophet ﷺ replied, "Praying on time." He asked again, "Which action does Allah love the most after that?" The Prophet ﷺ replied, "Treating your parents well." Then he asked a final time, "Which action is it after that?" The Prophet ﷺ replied, "Working in the path of Allah." (al-Bukhari and Muslim)

What do parents do for us?

Your parents looked after you when you were a baby. When you could not feed yourself, go to the toilet, walk, talk or do anything else. They helped you and gave you everything that you needed.

Your parents continue to look after you even now and they always make sure that you are happy and safe.

What should you do for your parents? You should do the following:

1 Listen to them and do as they say.

2 Do not be rude to them.

3 If you do not like something that they tell you to do, tell them in a nice way.

4 When parents are old we must look after them like they looked after us when we were young and could not do anything by ourselves.

5 Allah has ordered us to be kind to our parents.

6 Looking after parents when they are old leads to Paradise.

Allah teaches us in the Qur'an to pray for our parents. We should recite the following du`a:

$$\text{رَبِّ ارْحَمْهُمَا كَمَا رَبَّيَانِي صَغِيْرًا}$$

O my Lord! Have mercy on both of my parents as they brought me up in (my) childhood (with mercy).

Story: Serving Parents

One day, the Prophet ﷺ was sitting with his Companions. A man came up to him and said to the Prophet ﷺ, "I want to make a promise to you that I will travel to another country to spread the message of Islam and to defend Islam against its enemies, so that I can get great reward from Allah."

Although the man was asking permission from the Prophet ﷺ to do a very great and blessed duty for Islam

33

which would give him great reward from Allah, the Prophet ﷺ did not allow him to do this.

Instead the Prophet ﷺ asked him, "Are any of your parents alive?" The man replied, "Yes, actually both of them are alive."

The Prophet ﷺ asked him again, "Do you want to get great reward from Allah?" The man replied, "Yes." The Prophet ﷺ said, "Then in that case, go back to your parents and look after them and treat them well."

Although the man was asking to do one of the most difficult, important and rewarding acts in the sight of Allah. The Prophet ﷺ did not allow him to do that because his parents needed him more.

The moral of the story is that if your parents need you to look after them or help them then doing that is much better and rewarding in the sight of Allah than doing any other work.

Lesson 7

Taharah (The Ritual Purity)

Keeping clean is an important part of Islam. If we want to offer the Salah or touch the Qur'an, we must first be in a state of ritual purity. Being in a state of ritual purity means that we are clean and ready to worship Allah. In Arabic, we call this '**Taharah**' and it is a religious requirement.

One of the ways in which we can achieve a state of purity (Taharah) is by performing the Wudu' (the Ritual Ablution). Ablution is the act of washing oneself. As Muslims, we perform the ablution by washing our hands, face, arms and feet and we wipe over our heads with wet hands. By doing this, we achieve 'Taharah' and we then become ready to offer the Salah or to touch the Qur'an.

Without being in Taharah, we are not allowed to touch the Qur'an or offer the Salah. If we offer the Salah without Taharah, we would have to repeat it again. This is because the prayer is not accepted by Allah without

Taharah. Allah is pure, and He loves that which is pure. This shows us the importance of Taharah and why we should remain in Taharah all the time.

When we offer the Salah, we must first make sure that our bodies are clean. If there is any filth on our bodies, we should remove that first and wash that part of the body with water. After this we become ready to perform Wudu'. When we complete Wudu', we attain Taharah and we continue to remain in that pure state until we do one of the actions that break Wudu'.

While we are in the state of purity (Taharah), we can pray as much as we want, and we can touch the Qur'an. But if we break our Wudu', then we can only pray and touch the Qur'an if we redo our Wudu' again.

So, what are those things that break the Wudu'? They are the following things:

GOING TO THE TOILET
When we pass urine or stool, our Wudu' breaks and we are no longer in the state of purity (Taharah).

PASSING WIND
If we pass wind our Wudu' breaks, even if we do it by accident or we forget.

VOMITING
If we vomit, and we are not able to control the vomit because it is a lot, then our Wudu' is broken and it needs to be renewed.

SLEEPING
If we sleep lying down, it will nullify our state of purity (Taharah). However, if we fall asleep while offering the Salah, it does not break the Wudu'.

BLEEDING
If blood comes out of our body and it flows, it means our Wudu' is broken. The same is the case with pus (a white yellowish thick liquid)

LAUGHING ALOUD DURING THE SALAH
If you laugh during the Salah and it is loud enough to be heard, then you must do your Wudu' again and repeat your Salah.

BECOMING INSANE, LOSING CONSCIOUSNESS OR BECOMING DRUNK
In these situations, there is a change in our mental state, so it breaks the Wudu'

If any of the above happens to us, we would no longer be in a state of purity (Taharah). If we wanted to offer the Salah or touch the Qur'an, we would have to do Wudu' again.

Lesson 8

Sirah: Rebuilding of the Ka`bah

When Prophet Muhammad ﷺ was 35 years old, the Quraysh decided to rebuild the Ka`bah. The Quraysh were a tribe, which Prophet Muhammad ﷺ belonged to. There were many families in the Quraysh and they were all related to each other. The Quraysh were chosen by Allah to look after the Ka`bah, and they would give water to the people who used to visit it from places far and wide.

The Ka`bah is the House of Allah. It was built many thousands of years ago by Prophet Ibrahim ﷺ and his son Prophet Isma'il ﷺ. When the Quraysh decided to rebuild the Ka`bah, at that time it was not very high, and it had no roof, so they wanted to raise the walls to make them higher and to build a roof.

The Quraysh first started taking down the walls of the Ka`bah. They kept on removing one stone after another, until they reached the foundation.

The foundation contained large green coloured stones that looked like the humps of camels, and they were placed side by side. One of the men tried to pull them out, but as he tried to remove them a massive tremor shook Makkah. They took this as a sign that they should leave these stones as they are, and not to remove them.

The Quraysh then began to erect the walls and every family of the Quraysh helped in this task. Some of them gathered stones and others would place them on top of each other. They continued with their task, until the time came to place the 'Black Stone' back in its place.

The Black Stone (al-Hajar al-Aswad) is a special stone. It was brought down from Paradise (Jannah) by Angel Jibra'il ﷺ and was given to Prophet Ibrahim ﷺ. When it came down from Paradise, it was whiter than milk, but it turned black because of the sins and bad deeds of the people. Each clan wanted the special task of putting the Black Stone in its place.

As they were deciding who would do this special task, everyone started fighting and almost killed each other because they all wanted to do it. Then one of the people stood up and said, "O Quraysh! Let the first person who enters the Mosque in the morning decide this matter for you." They all agreed to this and waited.

As they were waiting, they were pleasantly surprised to see that the first person to enter the mosque in the morning was Prophet Muhammad ﷺ. When they saw him, they shouted, "It is Muhammad, the trustworthy. We are happy with him and we accept his decision."

After hearing what happened, Prophet Muhammad ﷺ asked them to bring a cloak. He placed the Black Stone in the middle of the cloak and asked a person from each family to hold one side of the cloak and to carry the Black

Stone together. They did as they were told, and they carried the Black Stone to the Ka`bah. When the Black Stone reached the Ka`bah's corner, the Prophet ﷺ picked up the Black Stone and fixed it in its place with his own hands.

In this way, Prophet Muhammad ﷺ stopped the fighting and killing within the Quraysh. He united the families and gave them all a chance to take part in putting the Black Stone in the Ka`bah's corner.

Allah had gifted Prophet Muhammad ﷺ with wisdom and gave him all of the things that are needed to be a great leader and a Prophet of Allah. His truthfulness and trustworthiness made him accepted by everyone

43

Lesson 9

Allah is Self-Sufficient

Allah is the Self-Sufficient. This means that He does not need anyone or anything.

Allah does not need any help from anyone. No one can help Allah because He does not need any help. It is us who needs Allah's help and it is Allah Who helps everybody.

When we were small, we could not walk or talk. Allah gave us food and water, and then we grew bigger and bigger. Every day we kept on growing taller and taller, and we are still growing. We need Allah's help to grow.

It is Allah Who made the food and water for us. If Allah did not make food or water, then we would not be alive. But Allah does not need food or water. He is the One Who made food and water for us.

Everything needs Allah. Even the food we eat and the water we drink need Allah. Food and water cannot make themselves. They need Allah to make them. If Allah did not make them, they would not exist.

Allah made everything for us. Allah is so Kind and Merciful that He wants us to have all these good things. These good things help us and keep us healthy and strong. Allah does not need anything He makes.

Everyone needs food to eat and water to drink. If we don't have them, it will make us become weak, and when we become weak, we die. We all need the food and water Allah created for us to stay alive. Food and water are Allah's creation.

Allah is the Creator and the One True God. He does not need anything, because He is the Self-Sufficient. If someone needs food, water and air to stay alive, it means he is not self-sufficient, and if someone is not self-sufficient, he cannot be God.

From the time of Prophet Adam ﷺ to the last human being before the Day of Judgement, every human being needs food, water and air to stay alive. No human being is self-sufficient; and so, no human being can be God.

Lesson 10

Two, Three and Four Unit Prayers

We have learnt the basic positions of the Salah (the Ritual Prayer) in their order and the things to be recited in each position. However, it is important for us to also know how to offer the prayer when there are different number of units. A unit of prayer in Arabic is called 'Rak`ah', and every prayer is made up of either two, three or four units.

In this lesson, we will learn how to offer the prayer if there are two, three or four units in the prayer.

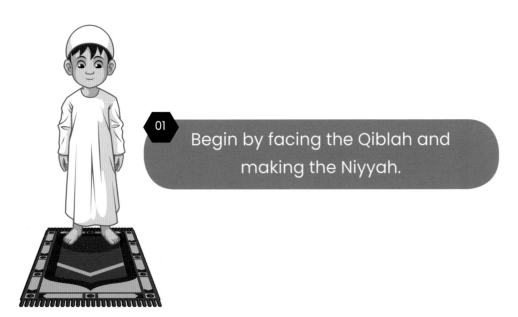

01

Begin by facing the Qiblah and making the Niyyah.

02

Perform the Takbir at-Tahrimah.

03

Perform the Qiyam
(the Standing Position).

Recite the Thana' (Praise of Allah), then the Ta`awwudh (Seeking Refuge in Allah) and then the Tasmiyah (In the Name of Allah). Then recite Surat al-Fatihah, followed by a short Surah.

04 Perform the Ruku'
(the Bowing Position)

05 Perform the Qawmah
(the Short Standing Position).

06 Perform the Sajdah
(the First Prostration
Position)

07 Perform the Jalsah
(the Short Sitting Position)

08 Perform the Sajdah
(the Second
Prostration Position)

This completes the first unit of the prayer.

09

Perform the Qiyam
(the Standing Position).

Recite the Tasmiyah (In the Name of Allah), then recite Surat al-Fatihah, followed by a short Surah.

10

Perform the Ruku'
(the Bowing Position)

11

Perform the Qawmah
(the Short Standing Position).

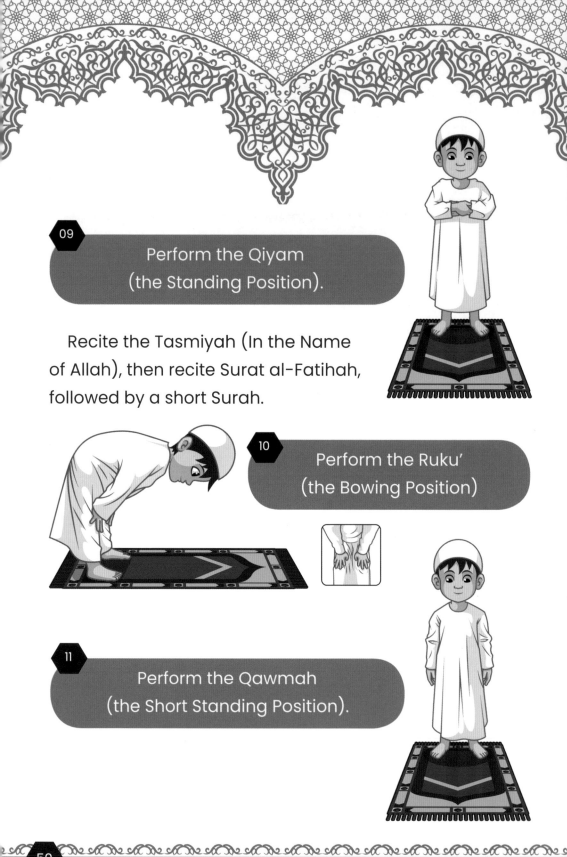

12 Perform the Sajdah (the First Prostration Position)

13 Perform the Jalsah (the Short Sitting Position)

14 Perform the Sajdah (the Second Prostration Position)

15 Perform the Qa'dah (the Sitting Position).

This completes the second unit of the prayer.

If you are offering the two-unit prayer, then complete the prayer from here.

If you are offering the three or four-unit prayer, recite the Tashahhud (the Bearing Testimony) and then return to the Qiyam (the Standing Position) to continue with the prayer.

Completing the Two-Unit Prayer:

16 Recite the Tashahhud (the Bearing Testimony), then the Salat Ibrahimiyyah (Abrahamic Salutation) followed by a Du`a.

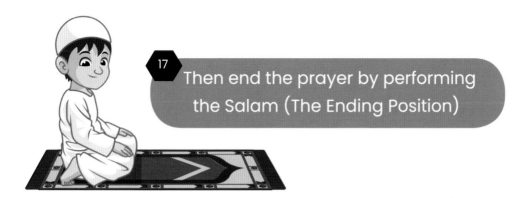

17 Then end the prayer by performing the Salam (The Ending Position)

This completes the two-unit prayer.

Continuing with the Three and Four Unit Prayers:

16 Perform the Qiyam (the Standing Position).

First recite the Tasmiyah (In the Name of Allah), then recite Surat al-Fatihah.

17 Perform the Ruku' (the Bowing Position)

18 Perform the Qawmah (the Short Standing Position).

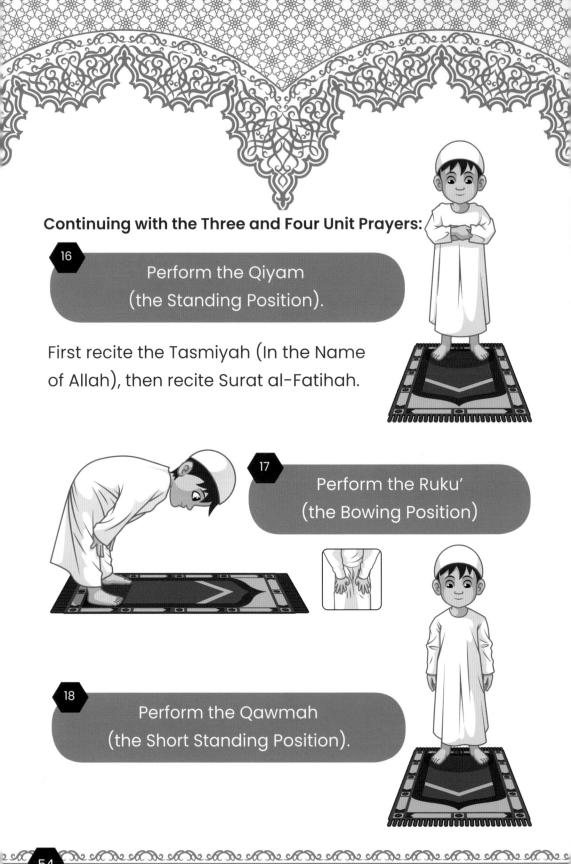

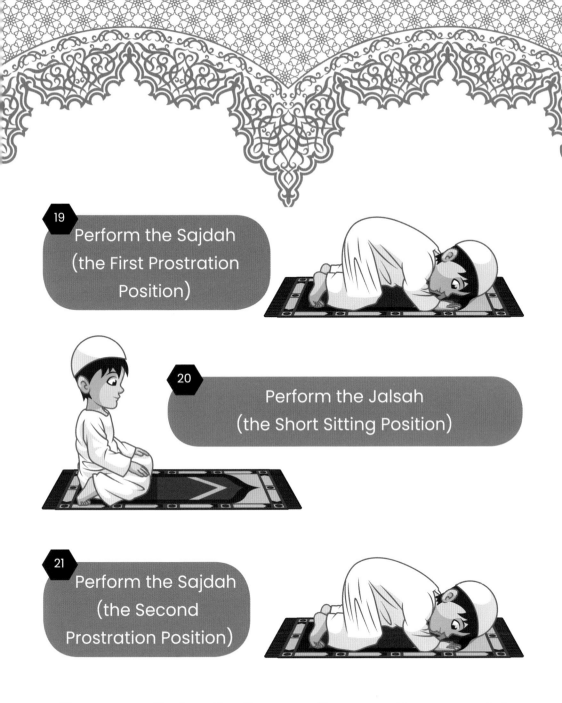

19 Perform the Sajdah (the First Prostration Position)

20 Perform the Jalsah (the Short Sitting Position)

21 Perform the Sajdah (the Second Prostration Position)

If you are offering the three-unit prayer, then complete the prayer from here.

If you are offering the four-unit prayer, then return to the Qiyam (the Standing Position) to continue with the prayer.

Completing the Three-Unit Prayer:

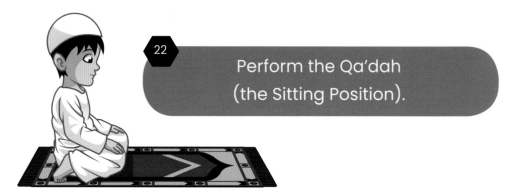

22 Perform the Qa'dah (the Sitting Position).

Recite the Tashahhud (the Bearing Testimony), then the Salat Ibrahimiyyah (Abrahamic Salutation) followed by a Du`a.

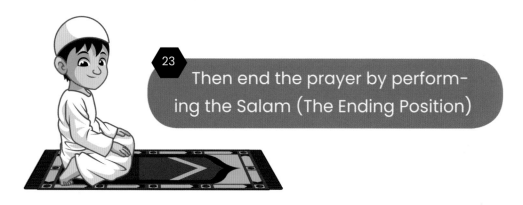

23 Then end the prayer by performing the Salam (The Ending Position)

This completes the three-unit prayer.

Continuing with the Four-Unit Prayer:

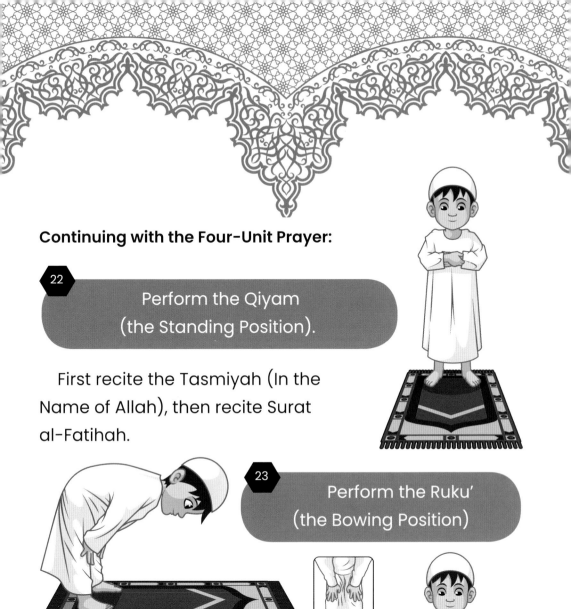

22 Perform the Qiyam (the Standing Position).

First recite the Tasmiyah (In the Name of Allah), then recite Surat al-Fatihah.

23 Perform the Ruku' (the Bowing Position)

24 Perform the Qawmah (the Short Standing Position).

25 Perform the Sajdah (the First Prostration Position)

26 Perform the Jalsah (the Short Sitting Position)

27 Perform the Sajdah (the Second Prostration Position)

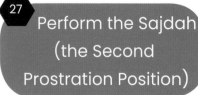

28 Perform the Qa'dah (the Sitting Position).

Recite the Tashahhud (the Bearing Testimony), then the Salat Ibrahimiyyah (Abrahamic Salutation) followed by a Du'a.

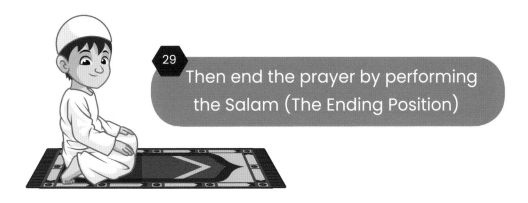

29 Then end the prayer by performing the Salam (The Ending Position)

This completes the four-unit prayer.

Lesson 11

Sirah: The Beginning of Revelation

When Prophet Muhammad ﷺ was nearly forty years old, he would go to a cave called Hira' to worship Allah. He liked to stay there alone and think about Allah. He would get upset seeing that his people were worshipping idols. The idols and statues could not help anyone, and they were made by people from stone and clay. The Prophet ﷺ would pray to Allah alone and he would stay away from the idols.

During this time, Prophet Muhammad ﷺ had special dreams. These special dreams were true dreams and they were a sign of Prophethood. Whatever Prophet Muhammad ﷺ would see in his dream, the next day it would come true, and happen just as he had seen it in his dream.

Whenever Prophet Muhammad ﷺ would walk outside, the stones and the trees would greet him and say: "Peace be upon you, O Messenger of Allah!" Many years later, the Prophet ﷺ said that he could still remember the stone that used to greet him and send him peace.

One night, during the month of Ramadan, the Prophet ﷺ was worshipping Allah in the cave Hira. Suddenly, Angel Jibra'il ﷺ appeared in the form of a man, and he said to Prophet Muhammad ﷺ, "Read!"

"I am not a reader!" said the Prophet ﷺ.

The angel hugged the Prophet ﷺ tightly, and again said, "Read!"

"I am not a reader" replied the Prophet ﷺ once more.

Again, the angel hugged the Prophet ﷺ tightly and said, "Read!"

"I am not a reader!" replied the Prophet ﷺ again.

Then, the angel said, "Read! In the name of your Lord, Who created!" The Prophet ﷺ recited the words and they were the first revelation sent by Allah through Angel Jibra`il ﷺ.

After the first revelation, Prophet Muhammad ﷺ quickly left the cave Hira' and climbed down the mountain. As he was climbing down, he saw Angel Jibra'il ﷺ in his true form, he did not look like a man anymore. Everywhere the Prophet ﷺ looked the angel was there. The angel was so big that it filled the skyline. "O Muhammad! You are the Prophet of Allah and I am Jibra'il," said the angel. This was the beginning of the Prophet's mission.

When the angel left, Prophet Muhammad ﷺ ran home to his beloved wife, Lady Khadijah. "Cover me! Cover me!" he told her. The Prophet ﷺ was frightened by what happened; the weight of the first revelation and his meeting with Angel Jibra'il ؑ came as a shock to him.

When Lady Khadijah covered the Prophet ﷺ she said, "Allah will never dishonour you. You look after your family and relatives; you help the poor and weak; you serve your guests kindly; and you help those who are in need."

Lady Khadijah knew that her husband was the Prophet of Allah. She went to her cousin Waraqah bin Nawfal and told him what had happened. Waraqah was a Christian and he knew about the books of Allah that came before the Qur'an.

"By Allah! The Angel of Revelation has come to Muhammad," said Waraqah bin Nawfal to Lady Khadijah, "it is the same angel that came to Prophet Musa ؑ. Muhammad is the Prophet of his people." Hearing these words, Lady Khadijah went home to Prophet Muhammad ﷺ and told him what Waraqah bin Nawfal said.

On the next day, Prophet Muhammad ﷺ went to the Ka`bah to perform the Tawaf. There he met Waraqah bin Nawfal, who asked him, "What did you see and hear?" The Prophet ﷺ told him what had happened in the cave and the meeting with Angel Jibra'il عليه السلام.

Hearing the story again, Waraqah bin Nawfal said to Prophet Muhammad ﷺ, "Your people will call you a liar and they will hurt you. They will drive you away and fight with you. Allah knows, if I will see that day or not, but I will help you." Waraqa bin Nawfal then kissed the Prophet's head and the Prophet ﷺ returned home.

The Prophet ﷺ knew he was the Prophet of Allah. He was not worried about the future, because he knew that Allah had a great future for him. This meeting with Angel Jibra'il عليه السلام and the first revelation from Allah confirmed the signs he witnessed earlier in his life that he was indeed the Prophet and Messenger of Allah.

Lesson 12

Belief in the Prophets

Allah created us so that we get to know Him. But we cannot know Him all by ourselves because as human beings we are weak. Our minds are not strong enough to know Allah's true nature or to find out about Allah's Beautiful Names, Perfect Attributes and Commands all by ourselves. We need Allah's help.

Allah wanted to guide us to Him because He loves us very much. He did this by sending us Prophets and Messengers. The Prophets and Messengers are Allah's chosen people. Allah chose them to help us so that they can tell us about Him. The Prophets and Messengers are the greatest teachers, and they were sent to guide us.

Had Allah not sent us Prophets and Messengers, we would not have known that Allah is the Most-Merciful and the Most Kind. We would not have known that after we die we will be rewarded by Allah for our good deeds and punished for our bad deeds, or that there is a Paradise and Hellfire. We would not have even known how to worship Allah properly!

We only know all of this because they were taught to us by the Prophets and Messengers. Allah spoke to the Prophets and Messengers and sent them His special messages, known as revelation. Some of the Prophets and Messengers were given holy books. These holy books guide people and tell them what is right and wrong.

Some of the Prophets and Messengers were given miracles. Miracles are special signs that the Prophets show so that people know that they are speaking the truth. The miracles performed by the Prophets came as a challenge to those who disbelieved in Allah. When the disbelievers rejected the miracles of the Prophets, they were afflicted with a great punishment for their rejection of Allah's signs.

The following are some examples of the famous miracles and great punishments that the disbelievers were afflicted with:

 Prophet Nuh ﷺ told his people not to worship idols and false gods. He warned them of the Great Flood. He built the Ark and when the punishment came, the disbelievers all drowned.

Prophet Ibrahim ﷺ was thrown into the Great Fire but the fire did not burn him. He put forward strong arguments to teach people that Allah is One and He has no partner.

Prophet Salih ﷺ was given the she-camel that came out of mountain. Some of the disbelievers decided to kill this special creation of Allah, so Allah sent a strong wind that destroyed the homes of the people of Thamud.

Prophet Musa ﷺ showed Pharaoh many signs. His staff turned into a Great Serpent and he parted the Red Sea. Allah punished Pharaoh by drowning him and his army.

Prophet `Isa ﷺ spoke in the cradle when he was a baby and he brought the dead back to life and cured the sick. He showed the Bani Isra'il these signs so that they may return to Allah and be sincere in their religion.

Prophet Muhammad ﷺ received the Qur'an, which the Arabs were unable to challenge due to the beauty and greatness of its language. The Qur'an is the greatest book of guidance and it tells us about Allah's Beautiful Names, Attributes and Commands.

We must love and respect all of the Prophets. They are Allah's special servants and they are our way of getting close to Allah. If there were no Prophets or Messengers, we would be lost and without guidance, and we would not have any good in this life or the next.

Lesson 13

The Units of the Five Prayers

Salah (the Ritual Prayer) is the **second pillar of Islam**. It is one of the most important things in the life of a Muslim. As Muslims, we must pray five times a day. When we pray we are connecting with Allah and speaking to Him. The purpose of the Salah is to worship Allah and to remember Him.

The Five Daily Prayers

Each of the five daily prayers are based on the prayer of one of the great Prophets and friends of Allah. They are acts of remembrance of Allah's special servants. By praying these five daily prayers, we walk in the footsteps of those blessed people.

For example, when Allah accepted Prophet Adam's repentance, Prophet Adam ﷺ offered two units of prayer to thank Allah in the morning. These two units of prayer in the morning became the Fajr prayer.

When Prophet Ibrahim ﷺ was asked to sacrifice his son, and he passed the test, he offered four units of prayer thanking Allah in the afternoon. These four units of prayer became the Zuhr prayer.

When `Uzayr woke up from his sleep after one hundred years, he offered four units of prayer in thankfulness in the late-afternoon. These four units became the `Asr prayer.

When Prophet Ya`qub ﷺ or Prophet Dawud ﷺ recovered from a long period of illness, they intended to offer four units of prayer to thank Allah, but they were unable to complete the fourth unit. Allah liked this prayer so much that He made it the three units of the Maghrib prayer.

When Prophet Yunus ﷺ came out of the belly of the whale after being there for forty days and nights, he offered four units of prayer in thankfulness in the night. This four-unit prayer became the `Isha' prayer (Ibn `Abidin and at-Tahawi).

All these five prayers have been gathered together for the Ummah of Prophet Muhammad ﷺ. We must perform these five daily prayers and know the different number of units for each prayer.

The following table shows the number of units for the five daily prayers.

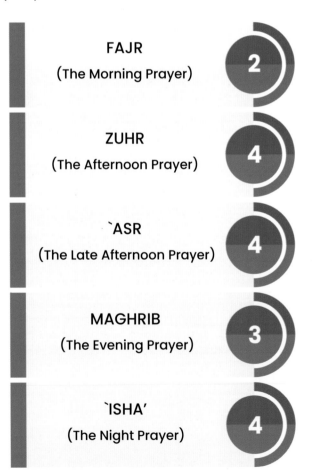

FAJR
(The Morning Prayer)
2

ZUHR
(The Afternoon Prayer)
4

`ASR
(The Late Afternoon Prayer)
4

MAGHRIB
(The Evening Prayer)
3

`ISHA'
(The Night Prayer)
4

The Fard and Witr (Wajib) Prayers

The above units of the five daily prayers are the most important and they are known as the '**Fard**' Prayers. Besides these, there are also other types of prayer that should be offered alongside the Fard. For example, after the four units of the `Isha' prayer, we must also offer three units of the Witr (Wajib) prayer. The **Witr (Wajib)** prayer is also important like the Fard prayer, and it cannot be missed.

If we miss either of the Fard or Witr (Wajib) prayer, we must make up those prayers in another time. This is known as '**Qada'**' (making up the missed prayer). The way to offer the Qada' is to offer the Fard and Witr (Wajib) prayers as soon as the time for that prayer has passed, before offering the next prayer.

The Sunnah Prayers

After the Fard and Witr (Wajib) prayers, there are the **Sunnah** prayers, and they are next in the order of importance. The Sunnah prayer is of two types: Sunnah Mu'akkadah, which are the emphasised Sunnah, and

the Sunnah Ghayr Mu'akkadah, which are the non-emphasised Sunnah.

Prophet Muhammad ﷺ always used to offer the Sunnah Mu'akkadah prayers and never missed them. He would sometimes miss the Sunnah Ghayr Mu'akkadah prayers, but they are both important and part of the Prophet's practice (Sunnah).

There are 12 units for the Sunnah Mu`akkadah prayers and they are: two units before Fajr, four units before Zuhr and two units after, and two units after both Maghrib and `Isha'. There are two Sunnah prayers that are Sunnah Ghayr Mu`akkadah, and they are the four units before both `Asr and `Isha'.

The Nafl Prayers

Then comes the '**Nafl**' prayer, which is voluntary. This means that we have a choice to either perform this prayer or to leave it. However, it is important to offer these prayers because they make up for the shortcoming in our other prayers. The Nafl prayers are all two units, and they are offered after the Sunnah Mu'akkadah prayers that come after the Fard prayer and after the Witr prayer.

Summary

The following table shows the units of the five daily prayers.

PRAYER	Sunnah	Fard	Sunnah	Nafl	Witr	Nafl
Fajr	2	2				
Zuhr	4	4	2	2		
`Asr	4	4				
Maghrib		3	2	2		
`Isha'	4	4	2	2	3	2

Lesson 14

The Final Message: The Qur'an

In the beginning, everyone belonged to the same religion. Prophet Adam ﷺ taught his children about the worship of Allah, the One True God. He told them about Paradise (Jannah) and the life hereafter. Everyone believed in this message and no one believed anything different.

As time went by, a long time after Prophet Adam ﷺ passed away, people began to forget Prophet Adam's message. Shaytan would whisper in their hearts to worship idols. He wanted them to forget about Allah and the life hereafter.

Allah did not want people to be misguided. So, He sent His Prophets and Messengers to remind people of the original message. To some of the Prophets, He gave holy books. These holy books had the original message which the people could read after their Prophet had passed away. They were a source of guidance and contained Allah's commands and rulings.

Some of the holy books were written in a very old language, which no one can understand today. Others got lost, because they were revealed a very long time ago. And some got changed by their followers and no longer had the original message in them.

Allah revealed one more book for the last time. This holy book was the Qur'an, and there will be no holy book after it. It is the final message. Allah has promised to keep the Qur'an safe from being lost or changed. He gave this holy book to Prophet Muhammad ﷺ to give to all people until the Last Day.

The Qur'an is a book of guidance and mercy. It contains stories, rulings and prayers. It is the greatest miracle of Prophet Muhammad ﷺ. The nature of its miracle is its beautiful language. The Qur'an came as a challenge to all of humanity to write a book like it; but after more than 1400 years no one has been able to write a book like the Qur'an.

All the miracles of the past Prophets have come and gone. They are no longer with us today. But Allah chose the Qur'an as a special miracle for Prophet Muhammad ﷺ. This miracle is still with us today, and it will be with us till the Day of Judgement.

Every day we can look at this miracle and learn from it. We can connect ourselves with the words of Allah and know the message which He sent to all the Prophets, from Prophet Adam to Prophet Muhammad (peace be upon them all).

The following are some important facts about the Qur'an:

It is Allah's speech, which was revealed to Prophet Muhammad ﷺ through the Angel Jibra'il عليه السلام.

It was revealed once in the heavens on al-Lawh al-Mahfuz during the month of Ramadan on a special night called the 'Night of Power' (Laylat al-Qadr).

It was then revealed to the Prophet ﷺ over a time of 23 years, several verses at a time. Not together as one book.

The word 'Qur'an' means recitation and it was revealed in the Arabic language.

05 It is divided into 30 parts known as 'Juz''.

06 It has chapters called 'Surah' and verses called 'Ayah'

07 There are 114 Surahs and 6,236 Ayahs.

08 The Surahs that were revealed before the Prophet's Hijrah (migration) to Madinah are known as Makki and those that were revealed after the Hijrah are known as Madani.

09 Some of the other names of the Qur'an are: al-Furqan (The Measure [Between Right and Wrong]); al-Kitab (Book); an-Nur (Light); al-Huda (Guidance); ar-Rahmah (Mercy); ash-Shifa' (Healing); and adh-Dhikr (Reminder).

Lesson 15

Sirah: The Beginning of the Prophet's Mission

Khadijah, the Prophet's wife, was the first person to become a Muslim after the Prophet ﷺ received the revelation from Angel Jibra'il ﷺ. She always stood by the Prophet's side and supported him in his mission. She encouraged the Prophet ﷺ and comforted him when times were hard. Allah honoured her and commanded the Prophet ﷺ to give her the happy message that she will receive a beautiful house in Paradise made of pearls.

After the revelation of the Qur'anic verse, *"Warn your family who are your nearest of kin,"* (ash-Shu`ara' 26:214), the Prophet ﷺ decided to invite his family and relatives to his house to tell them about Islam. The Prophet ﷺ called his younger cousin `Ali, who was a young boy at that time, and said, "Allah has commanded me to invite my family and relatives to Islam. So, prepare some meat and milk so that I can fulfil this duty to invite the Banu `Abd al-Muttalib to Islam."

When the Prophet's relatives gathered in his house, `Ali brought the food which they had prepared. The Prophet ﷺ took a piece of the meat, bit it and then placed it back into the plate. He told his relatives to eat in the name of Allah. The men started to eat and they all ate from the same plate until no one could eat anymore. `Ali said, "I could see no change in the plate except that it had been stirred by their hands. One man alone could have finished the food in that plate."

Then the Prophet ﷺ ordered `Ali to give them the milk to drink. So `Ali brought the cup of milk and the men drank to their fill, even though that one cup of milk was only enough for one person. After everyone had eaten and drunk until they were full, the Prophet ﷺ was about to talk to them and tell them about Islam. However, Abu Lahab interrupted the Prophet ﷺ and said, "Your host has put a spell on you." After hearing this, all the relatives left before the Prophet ﷺ could speak.

The next day the Prophet ﷺ told `Ali to prepare another meal. So, `Ali started making the same preparations as he made for the night before. After the meal, the Prophet ﷺ got up and spoke to his relatives. "O sons of `Abd al-Muttalib," he said, "I don't know any Arab who has come to his people with a message more honourable than mine. I bring you the best of this world and the next. Allah has commanded me to call you all to Islam. So, who among you will support me and be my brother and successor?"

There was silence among everyone. No one knew what to say. However, `Ali – the brave young boy – got up and said, "O Prophet of Allah, I will be your helper!" The Prophet ﷺ was happy with `Ali and put his hand on his back and said, "This is my brother and my successor among you. So, listen to him and obey him." Hearing this, the relatives all got up and they laughed.

In the beginning, the Prophet ﷺ called his family and friends to Islam in secret. After Khadijah, the Prophet's cousin `Ali, was the next person to accept Islam. He was then followed by Zayd bin Harithah, who was the Prophet's freed slave and adopted son. Abu Bakr, the Prophet's best friend, was next and he was the first among the men to

accept Islam. The Prophet ﷺ kept on inviting his family, relatives and friends to Islam in secret until a good number of them became Muslims and accepted his message.

During these early days, Angel Jibra'il ﷺ showed the Prophet ﷺ how to perform the Wudu' (ablution) and Salah (prayer). The Prophet ﷺ then taught this to his followers, and they all practised Islam in private. Some famous Companions of the Prophet ﷺ became Muslims in this time because of the hard work by Abu Bakr to spread the message of Islam. Some of the companions were: `Uthman bin `Affan, az-Zubayr bin al-`Awwam, `Abd ar-Rahman bin `Awf, Sa`d bin Abi Waqqas and Talhah bin `Ubayd Allah.

The Prophet ﷺ was very happy with Abu Bakr for his honesty and commitment to the cause of Islam. He said, "I did not call anyone to Islam except that they were a little unsure in accepting it – except for Abu Bakr, he did not have any feeling of being unsure in accepting what I mentioned to him." (al-Bayhaqi)

Lesson 16

The Sunnah and the Nafl Prayers

On the Day of Judgement, the first thing Allah will judge from our worship will be the Salah (the Ritual Prayer). If the Salah is complete then our accountability before Allah will be easy; but if our prayers are incomplete, then we will find ourselves in great difficulty.

The most important of the Salah are the Fard prayers, which are obligatory on all Muslims to pray. The next is the Witr prayer. If anyone misses the Fard or the Witr prayers, they have to make up these prayers and this is known as Qada'.

Allah will ask us about the Fard and Witr prayers, whether we performed them or not. If we did not perform them, then we will have to use some of our good deeds to make up for those missed prayers. If we did not offer them perfectly or with mistakes, Allah will look at our Sunnah and Nafl prayers to make up for those shortcomings.

This is why it is important to offer the Sunnah and Nafl prayers. By offering these prayers we make sure that when our prayers are judged by Allah, these extra prayers will help us to make up for the imperfections in our Fard prayers. We can pass the accountability on the Day of

Judgement by making sure our prayers are in order.

When it comes to offering the Sunnah and Nafl prayers, there are some differences with the Fard prayers. Some of these differences are mentioned below.

1 We can offer the Nafl prayers sitting down when we are tired, but the Fard prayers cannot be offered sitting down unless we are ill or cannot stand up.

2 We must specify the Fard and Witr prayers in our intention by saying that we are going to offer the Fard or Witr prayer. With the Nafl prayer, this is not necessary.

3 We recite a short Surah after Surat al-Fatihah in every unit (rak`ah) of the Sunnah and Nafl Prayers. Whereas, in the Fard prayer, we only recite a short Surah in the first two units of the prayer.

4 In the third unit (Rak'ah) of the Sunna and Nafl Prayers, we recite the Thana' (Praise of Allah) and the Ta`awwudh (Seeking Refuge in Allah), but we do not recite them in the Fard prayer.

5 The Fard prayers are offered at their fixed timing. The Nafl prayers can be offered at any time of the day.

However, there are certain times of the day when we are not allowed to offer the prayer, even if it is the Nafl prayer.

These timings are:

1. At sunrise

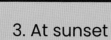

2. At midday

3. At sunset

How to Offer the Sunnah and Nafl Prayers

We begin by entering the prayer.

01

Begin by facing the Qiblah and making the Niyyah.

02

Perform the Takbir at-Tahrimah.

Once we start the prayer, the first unit begins.

03

Perform the Qiyam
(the Standing Position).

First recite the Thana' (Praise of Allah), then the Ta`awwudh (Seeking Refuge in Allah) and then the Tasmiyah (In the Name of Allah). Then recite Surat al-Fatihah, followed by a short Surah.

04

Perform the Ruku'
(the Bowing Position)

05

Perform the Qawmah
(the Short Standing Position).

06 Perform the Sajdah
(the First Prostration
Position)

07 Perform the Jalsah
(the Short Sitting Position)

08 Perform the Sajdah
(the Second
Prostration Position)

09

Then begin the next unit by performing the Qiyam (the Standing Position).

First recite the Tasmiyah (In the Name of Allah), then recite Surat al-Fatihah, followed by a short Surah.

10

Perform the Ruku' (the Bowing Position)

11

Perform the Qawmah (the Short Standing Position).

89

12 Perform the Sajdah (the First Prostration Position)

13 Perform the Jalsah (the Short Sitting Position)

14 Perform the Sajdah (the Second Prostration Position)

15 Perform the Qa'dah (the Sitting Position).

Recite the Tashahhud (the Bearing Testimony).

If you are offering the two-unit prayer, then complete the prayer from here.

If you are offering the four-unit prayer, then return to step 3 and complete the steps to the end.

Note: You can even offer 6, 8 and 10 units of Nafl prayer by returning to step 3 and continuing with the prayer.

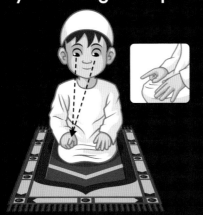

16

After the Tashahhud (the Bearing Testimony), recite the Salat Ibrahimiyyah (Abrahamic Salutation) followed by a Du`a.

17

Then end the prayer by performing the Salam (The Ending Position)

This completes the prayer.

Lesson 17

Sirah: The Open Invitation to Islam

The early Muslims first used to practise Islam privately in their homes. People would hear about Islam and would enter Islam in small groups. This lasted for three years, after which Allah commanded the Prophet ﷺ to invite the people of the Quraysh to Islam openly. Obeying Allah's command, Prophet Muhammad ﷺ climbed Mount Safa and called his tribe to accept Islam.

"O Quraysh!" called the Prophet ﷺ until all the people gathered together at Mount Safa to listen to him. "If I were to inform you that there were horsemen in this valley ready to attack you, would you believe me?"

"Yes! We have not heard you say anything except the truth," they all replied.

"Then be aware that I am a warner from Allah to warn you of a great punishment," Prophet Muhammad ﷺ told them.

When Abu Lahab heard this warning, he became angry. "May you perish!" he said to the Prophet ﷺ. "You gathered us here just to tell us this?" He then walked away. After this disrespectful act, Allah revealed a complete chapter in the Qur'an talking about Abu Lahab's punishment.

After Allah gave the command to invite people to Islam, the Muslims began to pray openly around Makkah. Every time they would pray the idol worshippers would call them names and use bad language, making fun of the way that they prayed. However, the Muslims, remained patient and would not listen to them. They continued to practice Islam and paid no attention to whatever the idol worshippers said to them.

But sometimes the idol worshippers would behave really badly towards the Muslims, so the Muslims reacted to them. They replied to their name-calling and stood up for themselves against their anger. Sometimes there would be arguments between them that would almost turn into fights. Once, a young man called Sa`d hit one of the idol worshippers with a camel's bone and hurt him quite badly. Allah commanded the Muslims to stay patient and to not fight or hurt anybody.

During these years, the Prophet ﷺ continued his mission to invite the idol worshippers to Islam. As the anger and unfriendliness against the Muslims got worse, a Companion called al-Arqam bin Abi al-Arqam said that his house could be used as a safe place. Here, the Muslims prayed to Allah in peace, away from the eyes of the idol worshippers. His house, which came to be known as 'Dar al-Arqam', was the first learning centre in Islam. In this house, the Prophet ﷺ taught his Companions the Qur'an and showed them how to pray and worship.

The first people to accept Islam were young people. Men and women from different tribes who became Muslims. The leaders from the Quraysh, which was the most powerful tribe in Makkah, were not happy with this new religion, because they saw it as a threat to their leadership. They wanted Abu Talib, the Prophet's uncle, to talk to the Prophet ﷺ and ask him not to speak against their gods or to call people to Islam. Abu Talib told them not to worry and that everything would be alright.

When the Quraysh saw that the Prophet ﷺ was not stopping his mission, they lost patience. They went to Abu Talib and said to him, "You hold a high and honourable position among us. We asked you to keep your nephew in place, but you have not done it yet. We will not let go of our ways or allow our gods to be rejected. Either make him stop or we will fight both of you." Then they left.

Abu Talib was worried by this. He then called the Prophet ﷺ and said to him, "O son of my brother, save me and save yourself. Do not put me in a situation that I cannot handle."

Hearing this, the Prophet ﷺ said with a sad voice, "By Allah, if they put the sun in my right hand and the moon in my left on the condition that I leave this mission, I will not leave it." Then the Prophet ﷺ fell silent.

After a while, he rose to his feet and was about to leave, but his uncle Abu Talib called him and said, "My dear nephew, go and say whatever you want, because by Allah I will never hand you over to anyone."

Abu Talib loved his nephew very dearly. He would never let anyone hurt him in any way. He vowed to protect his nephew to the end as he had protected him when he was a child.

Lesson 18

Adhan (The Call to Prayer)

The Adhan is the Muslim call to prayer. It is performed before each of the five daily prayers and its purpose is to let everyone know that it is time to pray.

Different religions use different methods to call people to pray. Bells, horns and fire have been used as the call to prayer, but in Islam, the Prophet Muhammad ﷺ chose the soothing melody of the human voice. The Adhan is a symbol of Islam and it is a beautiful and peaceful expression of the Islamic way of life.

There is an amazing story behind the Adhan. Allah gave this special gift to the Muslims through a true dream. It is reported that the Prophet Muhammad ﷺ wanted to call the Muslims to prayer. Someone said, "Hoist a flag at the time of prayer; when they see it, they will inform one another." The Prophet ﷺ, however, did not like this idea.

Someone suggested a horn, because the Jews used a horn, but the Prophet ﷺ did not like this idea as well. Another person suggested a bell like the Christians, but the Prophet ﷺ did not like this idea also. The Companion `Abd Allah bin Zayd was sitting in the meeting and he wished he could think of a good idea to tell the Prophet ﷺ. So, he went home and thought hard about the matter.

That night `Abd Allah bin Zayd had a dream in which he was taught the call to prayer. On the next day, he rushed to the Prophet Muhammad ﷺ and he told him about the true dream he had that night. He said, "O Messenger of Allah, I was between sleep and wakefulness. Suddenly a person came to me and taught me the call to prayer." When he narrated the dream, `Umar bin al-Khattab said that he had also seen it in his dream.

The Prophet Muhammad ﷺ was happy with this idea and he commanded his dear Companion Bilal, who was from Abyssinia (Africa), to call the people to prayer. Bilal had a beautiful voice and he was taught the words as it was taught to `Abd Allah bin Zayd. When Bilal made the call to prayer that day, he became the first 'Muezzin' in the history of Islam. A Muezzin is someone who makes the Muslim call to prayer; it comes from the Arabic word 'Mu`adhdhin'.

Let us walk in the footstep of the dear Companion Bilal and learn how to make the call to prayer in Islam.

We face the direction of the Ka`bah (this is known as Qiblah). We place our hands over our ears and then recite the following words loudly in our most beautiful voice.

اَللّٰهُ أَكْبَرُ اَللّٰهُ أَكْبَرُ

Allah is the greatest. Allah is the greatest.

اَللّٰهُ أَكْبَرُ اَللّٰهُ أَكْبَرُ

Allah is the greatest. Allah is the greatest.

أَشْهَدُ أَنْ لَّا إِلَهَ إِلَّا اللّٰهُ ، أَشْهَدُ أَنْ لَّا إِلَهَ إِلَّا اللّٰهُ

I bear witness there is no god but Allah.
I bear witness there is no god but Allah.

أَشْهَدُ أَنَّ مُحَمَّدًا رَّسُولُ اللّٰهِ ، أَشْهَدُ أَنَّ مُحَمَّدًا رَّسُولُ اللّٰهِ

I bear witness that Muhammad is the Messenger of Allah.
I bear witness that Muhammad is the Messenger of Allah.

Then turning the head to the right side, say:

حَيَّ عَلَى الصَّلَاةِ ، حَيَّ عَلَى الصَّلَاةِ.

Come to the Prayer. Come to the Prayer.

Then turning the head to the left side, say:

حَيَّ عَلَى الْفَلَاحِ ، حَيَّ عَلَى الْفَلَاحِ

Come to Success. Come to Success.

Then facing the Qiblah, say:

اَللّٰهُ أَكْبَرُ ، اَللّٰهُ أَكْبَرُ

Allah is the greatest. Allah is the greatest.

لَا إِلَهَ إِلَّا اللّٰهُ.

There is no god but Allah.

How to Perform the Adhan for the Fajr Prayer?

There is an additional phrase in the Fajr (Dawn) prayer. After saying 'Hayya `alal-Falaah; Hayya `alal-Falaah', we turn the face back to the Qiblah, and we say the following phrase:

اَلصَّلَاةُ خَيْرٌ مِّنَ النَّوْمِ ، اَلصَّلَاةُ خَيْرٌ مِّنَ النَّوْمِ

Prayer is better than sleep. Prayer is better than sleep.

How to Perform the Iqamah?

The Iqamah is recited before the start of the congregational prayer. Unlike the Adhan, it is recited quickly and only loud enough to be heard by people who are nearby. It used to be recited when the Prophet Muhammad ﷺ entered the mosque to lead the prayer, and thus it was an announcement for the Companions to get up for the Prophet ﷺ and to make the rows.

The Iqamah is recited with the same words as the Adhan, except that after saying 'Hayya `alal-Falaah; Hayya `alal-Falaah', the following words are recited:

قَدْ قَامَتِ الصَّلَاةُ، قَدْ قَامَتِ الصَّلَاةُ

The Prayer has begun. The Prayer has begun.

Unlike the Adhan, the head is not turned to the left or right at any time during the Iqamah.

What to do When Listening to the Adhan?

When the Adhan is being recited remain silent and listen to the Muezzin. Every time the Muezzin completes a statement, repeat it quietly after him. For example, when the Muezzin says, 'Allaahu Akbar; Allaahu Akbar', you say 'Allaahu Akbar; Allaahu Akbar'. This is to be done for the whole Adhan.

There is an exception, however. When the Muezzin says, 'Hayya `alas-Salaah; Hayya `alas-Salaah' or 'Hayya `alal-Falaah; Hayya `alal-Falaah', the following invocation should be recited:

لَا حَوْلَ وَلَا قُوَّةَ إِلَّا بِاللهِ ، لَا حَوْلَ وَلَا قُوَّةَ إِلَّا بِاللهِ

There is no power or might except with Allah.
There is no power or might except with Allah.

The Du`a After Adhan

After the Muezzin completes the Adhan, we recite the following Du`a:

اَللّٰهُمَّ رَبَّ هٰذِهِ الدَّعْوَةِ التَّامَّةِ وَالصَّلَاةِ الْقَائِمَةِ آتِ مُحَمَّدَا نِ الْوَسِيلَةَ وَالْفَضِيلَةَ وَالدَّرَجَةَ الرَّفِيْعَةَ وَابْعَثْهُ مَقَامًا مَّحْمُوْدَا نِ الَّذِيْ وَعَدْتَّهُ. وَارْزُقْنَا شَفَاعَتَهُ يَوْمَ الْقِيَامَةِ. إِنَّكَ لَا تُخْلِفُ الْمِيْعَادَ.

O Allah! Lord of this complete call and established prayer, give Muhammad the position and honour, and give him the praised station that You have promised. Grant us his intercession on the Day of Judgement. Indeed, You do not break Your promise.

It is recommended to recite Salawat on the Prophet Muhammad ﷺ after the Adhan. It is also recommended to supplicate to Allah in the time between the Adhan and the Iqamah, as it is one of the times when the supplication (du`a) is not rejected (Abu Dawud).

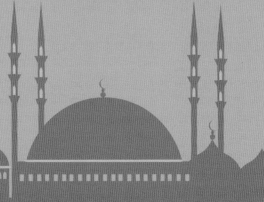

Lesson 19

The Day of Judgement

Allah wanted to guide people to the right way, so He chose some very special people to become His Prophets and Messengers. These Prophets and Messengers were given revelation by Allah. The revelation contained very important messages about our life and what will happen to us after we die.

One of the most important messages that was given to us by the Prophets and Messengers was about the Day of Judgement. Allah told His Prophets and Messengers to tell their people that one day, after they die, Allah will raise them from their graves and make them stand before Him on a very important day called 'the Day of Judgement'.

Without the Prophets, we would not have known about this important day. Prophet Muhammad ﷺ taught us that all people, from the first people since the time of Prophet Adam ﷺ until the last, will be gathered together in front of Allah on the Day of Judgement. This day will be our meeting with Allah. Allah will look at our deeds and He will judge us to see who amongst us did good deeds and who did bad.

On the Day of Judgement, there will be a scale and our deeds will be weighed. Our good deeds will be put on one side of the scale and our bad deeds on the other side. Then they will be weighed. If the good side is heavier than the bad, then the person will enter Heaven. But if the bad side is heavier, then the person will be taken to the Hellfire to be punished.

Prophet Muhammad ﷺ taught us many of the Signs of the Day of Judgement. These signs are the events that will take place in the future and which will be a reminder for us that the Day of Judgement is getting closer and closer.

Some of the Signs of the Day of Judgement which Prophet Muhammad ﷺ told us about are:

People who used to be poor and herd goats will compete with one another to build tall buildings.
(al-Bukhari and Muslim)

The buildings of Makkah will rise over the mountains.
(Ibn Abi Shaybah)

105

There will be less knowledge and more ignorance.

(al-Bukhari)

There will be many earthquakes and natural disasters.

(at-Tabarani)

People will believe the liars and they will disbelieve the truthful.

(Ibn Majah)

There will be a lot of killing.

(Ibn Majah)

In the Qur'an, the Day of Judgement (Yawm al-Qiyamah) has many names.

Some of them are:

AS-SA`AH (THE HOUR)

The Day of Judgement will come at an unknown time in the future.

AL-YAWM AL-AKHIR (THE LAST DAY)

It is the final day. There will not be another day after it.

YAWM AL-BA`TH (THE DAY OF RESURRECTION)

On this day, Allah will bring the dead back to life.

YAWM AL-HASHR (THE DAY OF GATHERING)

This is the day when Allah will gather all the people together to stand before Him.

YAWM AL-HISAB (THE DAY OF RECKONING)

It is the day when everyone's deeds will be weighed on the scales.

YAWM AD-DIN (THE DAY OF RECOMPENSE)

Allah will reward or punish everyone for their deeds on this day.

In the Arabic language, when something is important, it will have many names to describe it. All of these names of the Day of the Judgement show the important events that will take place on that day.

Lesson 20

Sirah: The Quraysh Campaign Against Islam

The people of Quraysh were well respected and powerful among the Arabs. They were the guardians of the Ka`bah and the well of Zamzam and the caretakers of the pilgrims. They were very welcoming and took good care of their guests, who came from far away to visit the Sacred House of Allah.

Even though people worshipped idols, the Ka`bah was still special, and pilgrims used to visit it. However, the Quraysh were scared that Islam would damage their good name among the Arabs. So, they decided to hold a meeting to discuss what to do when the pilgrims arrived in Makkah for the pilgrimage that year.

The Quraysh gathered together and Walid bin al-Mughirah, who was the eldest, started the meeting. "O Quraysh!" said Walid, "it is the time of Pilgrimage and people from the Arab tribes will come to you. Some of them have heard about Muhammad's message. So, let us agree on what we will say to them about him."

"O Abu `Abd ash-Shams! You tell us what to say so that

we can all agree," the Quraysh exclaimed.

"No, you all say what you think, and I will listen," Walid told them.

"We say he is a fortune-teller," they said.

"No, he is not a fortune-teller," he replied. "We have seen fortune-tellers. What he says is not like the mumbling of the fortune-teller or their rhyming style."

"We say he is a mad-man," they said.

"No, he is not a mad-man," he replied. "We have seen mad-men and we know them. He doesn't suffer from the signs of madness on his body. He doesn't have sudden attacks of choking. He doesn't lose control of his body and he doesn't talk to himself."

"We say then that he is a poet," they said.

"No, he is not a poet," he replied. "We know poetry and the many rhymes and beats. He is not a poet."

"Then let's say he is a sorcerer," they said.

"He is not a sorcerer," Walid replied. "We have seen the sorcerers and their sorcery. He does not make knots or blow into them."

"O Abu `Abd ash-Shams! What should we say then?" they exclaimed.

Walid said, "There is nothing that you can say because everyone will know it's not true. The closest thing that you can say about him is that he is a sorcerer: his message separates a son from his father, a man from his wife, a brother from his brother, and a person from his family."

The Quraysh agreed on this one thing to say against the Prophet ﷺ. They kept an eye on all the roads leading into Makkah. Every time a group of people came, they would go out to meet them. They would then warn them about the Prophet ﷺ and tell them the false news that they all agreed on, that he was a sorcerer and told people to stay away from him.

The Quraysh thought they were stopping people from learning about Islam, however, they did not realise that by doing this they were actually spreading the Prophet's message to all the tribes in Arabia. Some people, who were interested in the Prophet's message, decided to listen to him for themselves so they went to him, and others who were told the false news wanted to know more and they also went to meet the Prophet ﷺ. People from everywhere came to hear the Prophet ﷺ speak and some of them even accepted his message, taking the message of Islam back with them to their tribes.

One of these groups of people were from a small desert town called Yathrib. They were a group of idol worshippers belonging to the Aws and Khazraj tribes. In Yathrib the tribes were always fighting with each other, and the people were fed up and were looking for a way out of their difficult situation. They heard about the Prophet ﷺ and believed that he might be able to help them.

The Aws and the Khazraj tribes learned about the coming of the Prophet ﷺ from the Jews of Yathrib. So, when news came from Makkah of the appearance of a Prophet who called to the worship of the One God, the Arabs in Yathrib took interest in it and they wanted to meet the man who was known as a Prophet.

Lesson 21

Actions that Nullify the Prayer

The Salah (the Ritual Prayer) is the central pillar of Islam. Five times a day we take out time from our day to worship Allah. We must remember that when we pray we are standing before Allah and praying to Him. So, it is important that we concentrate on our prayer.

Before we start the Salah, we should check the following things are in place first:

> We should make sure that our body, clothes and the place of prayer are all clean and free from filth.

> We should make sure that we are dressed properly with good, respectable clothing which covers our body properly.

> We should face the Qiblah.

We should make the intention (niyyah).

We must be certain that the time for the prayer has started and there is enough time to offer the Salah.

Putting these things in place and paying attention to them will help us to prepare for the prayer.

The Salah begins from the 'Takbir at-Tahrimah' and it ends with the 'Salam'. During this time, we are in the state of the prayer and we must be cautious not to do something that will nullify it.

When we nullify the prayer, it means that we have broken the prayer. If the Salah is nullified, it must be offered again. So, what are the things that nullify the prayer?

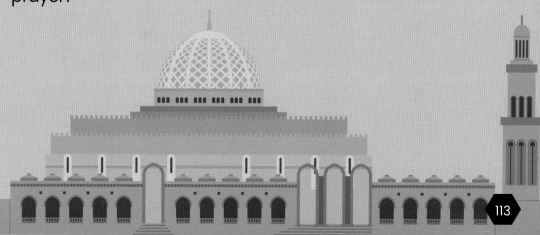

They are the following things:

1. BREAKING THE WUDU'

If a person is no longer in a state of purity (Taharah) because he or she broke their Wudu', then it would nullify the Salah.

2. TALKING

It is not permitted to speak to any person while offering the Salah. During the prayer, we must remain silent and not talk; we must concentrate on our prayer and only recite from the Qur'an or remember Allah.

If someone gives you Salam, you are not allowed to reply to their greeting.

If someone sneezes, and you reply to them by saying 'Yarhama-kallaah', it would nullify the Salah (the Ritual Prayer). Even if you say something by accident, it would nullify your Salah, and you will need to repeat it.

3. MAKING NOISES

Groaning, moaning and making noises nullify the Salah (the Ritual Prayer). In the same way, clearing the throat and saying 'ahem' without a valid reason or need also nullifies the Salah.

4. EATING OR DRINKING

It is not permitted to eat or drink anything during the Salah. In this sense, the Salah is like fasting, as we are not allowed to eat or drink.

If we have a bubble gum in our mouth or a sweet, we must spit it out and throw it in the bin and start the prayer with our mouth empty.

If you have eaten some food, it is good to rinse your mouth first.

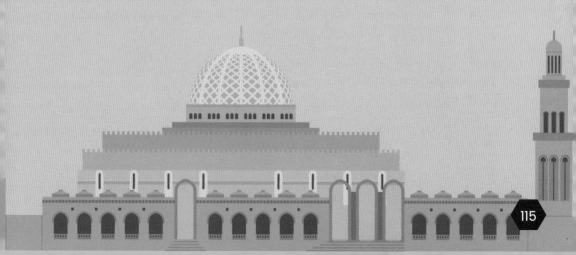

5. TURNING AWAY FROM THE QIBLAH

When we pray, we must concentrate on our prayer. We must not look around and be distracted from worshipping Allah. We should keep our gaze fixed to the ground at the place where our head does the prostration.

Throughout the prayer, we must keep our chest facing the Qiblah and not move it away from that direction. If we turn our chest away from the Qiblah, it would nullify our Salah.

6. FIDGETING AND PLAYING AROUND

Making three big movements in a row will break the prayer. If someone fidgets or plays around during the Salah such

that an onlooker will think that they are not praying, then it would nullify the prayer, and the person would have to repeat it again.

7. END OF THE PRAYER TIME
If a person is offering the Salah and the time of the prayer comes to an end, the prayer will be nullified, and the person will have to make up the prayer as Qada'.

8. MISSING ONE OF THE PILLARS OF THE SALAH
If someone misses the recitation of the Qur'an, the ruku` (the bowing position) or one of the Sajdahs (the prostration position) or any other pillar of the Salah, and the person does not make up for it before the prayer ends, then the Salah will be nullified.

Lesson 22

Sirah: Hamzah Accepts Islam

Even though the Quraysh tried their best to stop the message of the Prophet ﷺ, Islam was growing stronger day by day. Most of the people who became Muslims were young, the poor and the slaves. The leaders of the Quraysh did not accept Islam because they were scared that if Islam became powerful then they would lose their own power in Makkah.

The leaders of the Quraysh would make fun of the Prophet ﷺ and would say hateful things to him.

Once, Abu Jahl, who was one of the nastiest enemies of Islam, saw the Prophet ﷺ, sitting near the Ka`bah. So, he went up to the Prophet ﷺ and disrespected him by saying very bad words. But the Prophet ﷺ did not reply to him and remained silent.

After doing this, Abu Jahl turned his back to the Prophet ﷺ and went to join the other leaders of the Quraysh. The Prophet ﷺ remained sitting at his place for some time and then he got up and went home.

A slave-girl from the house of `Abd Allah bin Jada`an heard what had happened from inside her home. She felt sorry for the Prophet ﷺ and she did not want Abu Jahl to get away with it.

While all this was happening, the Prophet's uncle Hamzah was returning home from his hunting trip. Hamzah would always go to the Ka`bah first and pay his respect before going home to his family.

As he was going to the Ka`bah, the slave girl said to him, "O Abu Umarah! If only you had seen how your nephew Muhammad was treated by Abu Jahl; he was just sitting here quietly when Abu Jahl disrespected him very badly."

Hamzah became very angry when he heard this, and he went straight to where the Quraysh were sitting and stood above Abu Jahl. He raised his bow and brought it down with all his strength on Abu Jahl's back. "Will you insult him," Hamzah said, "now that I am part of his religion, and I believe what he believes. Hit me back if you dare." Some young people got up to help Abu Jahl, but Abu Jahl told them all to back down, because he knew that what he did was wrong. "Leave Abu Umarah alone," said Abu Jahl, "for by Allah I did insult his nephew."

The Quraysh would often treat the Prophet ﷺ badly and they even used to violently attack him. On one occasion, while the Prophet ﷺ was praying and prostrating (doing Sajdah) to Allah, `Uqbah bin Abi Mu`ayt took some guts from a camel and dropped them on the Prophet's back. The Prophet ﷺ remained prostrating to Allah even though the Quraysh were disrespecting and making fun of him.

Fatimah, the Prophet's youngest daughter, ran to her father to remove the filth from his back. She was very upset by this and was crying. But the Prophet ﷺ comforted her and said, "Don't cry my daughter. Indeed, Allah will make your father win."

The Quraysh wanted the Muslims to stop following the Prophet ﷺ. That is why they would do many bad things to try and make the Prophet ﷺ look bad so that people would stop believing in Islam. They tried everything that they could to stop the Prophet ﷺ.

They even tried to bribe the Prophet ﷺ. The Quraysh promised to make the Prophet ﷺ their king and offered him so much money that he would become the richest man in Makkah. But the Prophet ﷺ refused their offer and told them that he would not stop his mission to call people to Allah.

The Quraysh wanted to keep worshipping their gods and they did not want to lose their power, so they suggested to the Prophet ﷺ that they will worship Allah for one year, and then he would worship their gods the next year. They said, "If the Lord that you worship proves to be better than ours, then it will be much better for us, but if our gods prove to be better than yours, then we would have helped you."

When they said this, Allah revealed a complete chapter of the Qur'an to the Prophet ﷺ in reply to this idea from the Quraysh. Allah said: "*[O Prophet!] Say: 'O disbelievers! I do not worship those (idols) that you worship, nor do you worship (the Lord) Whom I worship. And I shall never worship those (idols) that you worship, nor will you (ever) worship (the Lord) Whom I worship. (So) you have your religion, and I have my Religion.'*" (al-Kafirun 109:1-6)

Lesson 23

The Third Pillar: Fasting and Ramadan

Fasting is a special and important part of the life of a Muslim. It is the third pillar of Islam. Fasting means that we do not eat or drink from dawn to sunset.

We fast in the holy month of **Ramadan**, which is the 9th month of the Muslim lunar calendar. Fasting in this holy month is obligatory on all Muslims; however, it is not obligatory on children who are in primary school.

During the holy month of Ramadan, we wake up before dawn and we have a special meal called '**Suhur**' (the pre-dawn meal). The Prophet Muhammad ﷺ told us to partake in the 'Suhur' (the pre-dawn meal) as it has blessings.

When the first rays of the sunlight can be seen on the horizon, we begin our fast. It starts the same time when the Fajr prayer begins. We fast during the daylight hours from dawn to sunset.

While we are fasting, we do not eat or drink anything. Eating and drinking break the fast. Even if we put something in our mouth and we swallow it by accident our fast breaks! Swallowing something, even if it is not food, will break the fast too. So, it is important to be mindful and not to put things in our mouth carelessly.

If you eat or drink something because you forgot that you were fasting, your fast does not break. In this situation, you are excused. Allah wanted you to forget because He wanted you to have something to eat and drink! You should continue fasting like normal and not eat anything else.

When we fast, we do not only fast with the **stomach**. Fasting is not just about staying away from food and drink. We must also fast with our eyes, ears, tongues and hands!

- We fast with our **eyes** by not looking at bad things. We should only look at those things that help us to get closer to Allah and become better human beings.

- We fast with our **ears** by not listening to bad words. During the month of Ramadan, we should listen to the recitation of the Qur'an, Nashids in praise of the Prophet ﷺ and lectures that help us increase our knowledge.

- We fast with our **tongues** by not saying anything bad. We should never swear or say harsh things to other people. If we fast, but we say horrible things to others, what would be the point of our fasts? Because the purpose of fasting is to become better people.

☐ We fast with our **hands** by making sure we do not hurt anybody. We should use our body only for good things and doing good deeds. In the month of Ramadan, we need to increase our good deeds by helping others and doing acts of charity.

When the sun sets in the evening, it is time for the fasting person to break the fast. Breaking the fast is called '**Iftar**'. Allah has promised two delights for the fasting person: the first is the delight of breaking the fast with delicious food; and the second is the meeting with Allah.

Ramadan is a very special month for Muslims. In this month, Allah gives us more rewards than in any other month, and every night He forgives people and frees them from the Hellfire. When this holy month starts the doors of Paradise are opened and the doors of the Hellfire are closed. The devils are chained and locked up. From one Ramadan to the next our minor sins are forgiven.

Throughout the month of Ramadan, we should increase our Dhikr (remembrance of Allah), Salat `ala an-Nabi ﷺ (salutation on the Prophet ﷺ), acts of charity and the recitation of the Qur'an. Every night we should join the **Tarawih** prayer. This is a special prayer which is 20 units in total and it is offered two units at a time. During the month of Ramadan, the whole Qur'an is recited during this prayer.

In the last ten days of Ramadan, Muslims stay in the mosque for a spiritual retreat. This retreat is known as '**I`tikaf**'. During these ten days, we seek a special night which is better than a thousand months. This special night is known as the '**Night of Power**' (**Laylat al-Qadr**) and it is the night when the Qur'an was revealed. Muslims seek this night from the odd nights from these last ten days. It is a night of forgiveness and Allah's mercy.

Lesson 24

Paradise and Hell

Allah knows everything that we do. On the Day of Judgement, Allah will ask us about our actions. If we did good deeds, we will be rewarded. But if we did bad deeds, we will be punished.

If a person's good deeds are more than their bad deeds, they will go to a special place called Paradise (Jannah).

Paradise (Jannah) is a very beautiful place, nobody has ever seen anything like it before. There is nothing in this world like it.

In Paradise (Jannah), no one will die or become old. Everyone will be young, healthy and very beautiful. Everyone will live forever and not be scared of anything or have any worry. Allah will never be angry with its people, and He will always be happy with them.

The Prophet Muhammad ﷺ told us that the first group of people who enter Paradise (Jannah) will appear like the full moon. The second group will appear like the most beautiful bright star in the night sky.

The Prophet ﷺ also told us that Allah has prepared for its people such beautiful and amazing things that the eyes have never seen, or the ears have never heard of. There will be such things there that have not come to the mind of any person.

In Paradise (Jannah) everything will be pure and good, and people will get everything that they want. And there will be markets where people can take whatever they want without having to pay for it. The soil will smell of musk (a sweet-smelling perfume) and the palaces will be made from bricks of gold. The people will ride animals that are fast as lightening and that can fly.

The greatest blessing in Paradise (Jannah) will be to see Allah. The people of Paradise will gather together, and they will remember Allah. During that gathering, all the people of Paradise will see Allah for the first time. Allah will talk to every person and give them His greetings of peace, and He will ask every person if they are happy with all the good things they have received.

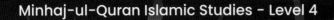

Hell (Jahannum), on the other hand, will be a very terrifying place. It is where wicked people will go as a punishment from Allah for their bad deeds.

People who disobey Allah will not see Him or talk to Him. In Hell (Jahannum) they will be lonely and hungry, and their punishment will not stop. They will stay there until Allah decides for them to leave or He forgives them.

The people of Hell will call out to Allah to help them, but Allah will not talk to them. He will not listen to what they want. The people of Hell will be ignored by all the angels and the people of Heaven. They will not have anything, not even water to drink.

Their punishment will continue forever, and it will not stop. They will be made to eat plants with sharp thorns and drink boiling hot water mixed with blood and pus. The angels who will punish them all day and night will

be deaf and blind, and they will not hear their screams or cries. They will keep on punishing the people of the Hellfire as they have been ordered by Allah.

The people of the Hellfire will be full of remorse and sadness. They will wish they had listened to the Prophets and Messengers and not disbelieved in them. The people who believed in Allah and His Prophets will ask the people of the Hellfire if Allah's promise has come true. The people of the Hellfire will admit that they were wrong, but their belief on that day will not be of any benefit to them.

May Allah protect us from the Hellfire and grant us His company in Paradise (Jannah) forever. Amin!

Lesson 25

The Fourth Pillar: Zakah

Zakah is the fourth pillar of Islam. Zakah means to give a small part of your money to the poor and needy people. The main reason that Muslims give Zakah is to help those people who are in need. We share our money with others so that we can help them.

Having money is a big responsibility. We do not own our wealth. Our wealth belongs to Allah. We must use it as He has commanded us to use it. Whatever money Allah gives us, there is a share of it that we must give to other people who need it more. By sharing our money with others, it

helps to purify us from greed and selfishness. It also cleans our wealth and puts more blessings in it.

Hiding your wealth and not spending it on people who need it is a big sin. Zakah is a way of sharing money and helping to make sure that people who need it are looked after. It teaches us to not be greedy and to think about others. When we give some of our money to others, it makes us more caring and a better human being. We make sure that no one is left poor in our society, and this helps society to become better.

The Zakah is paid only from the money we have saved over the year, and so it is from our spare money which we do not need. By sharing the extra money that we have, we help fulfil the needs of others. If everyone gives a part of their savings to those that are less well off, we make everyone better off as there is more money to go around for everyone to buy the things they need.

The Zakah is one of the ways of being thankful to Allah for all His blessings. By sharing our wealth, we are thinking of Allah. It is one of the ways of recognising all the good things Allah has given you, because you are sharing Allah's blessings with others. When we show appreciation for Allah's blessings in this way, Allah gives us more in return. He keeps bad times away from us and He forgives our sins and mistakes.

> We must give the Zakah once every year. We give it by taking a very small amount out of our savings. **The rate of Zakah is 2.5%**. This is equal to giving £1 from every £40 we have saved. So, if we had £100 in our savings, we give only £2.50 to the poor and needy as Zakah. In other words, from every £40 we have saved, we give £1 as Zakah and we keep £39 to ourselves! And yet if we do this, Allah will be happy with us and give us blessings in our wealth.

As Muslims, we should do as much charity as we can. The Zakah is an obligatory act which all Muslim adults have to do. It is only the least amount of money we must give to the poor and needy people. But all Muslims, young and old, should give as much charity as they can.

Charity in Arabic is called '**Sadaqah**', and it is optional. Allah has not put any limit on Sadaqah. So, we can do as much Sadaqah as we want to. It is something we can do every day, and it is more than just giving money to the poor and needy.

Giving money to the poor and needy people is one form of Sadaqah, but it is not the only form. For example, the following things are all examples of 'Sadaqah' (charity in Islam):

Feeding others and sharing our food with our neighbours.

Giving a thirsty person water to drink.

Sharing our snacks and sweets with our friends.

Gifting someone a nice present.

Helping our parents and family with the house chores.

Helping someone in need.

Teaching someone or helping a friend with their homework.

Smiling when meeting someone.

Making someone happy.

Speaking kind words to others.

Building a mosque or a school.

Planting a tree.

Lesson 26

Sirah: The Migration to Abyssinia

The Quraysh started to treat the Muslims even more harshly because they knew that the Prophet ﷺ would not stop telling people about the message of Allah. They mainly attacked the poor and weak Muslims because they knew that none of the powerful leaders were on their side. If any of their young family members embraced Islam, they would lock them up in their homes and not give them any food for many days until they decided to leave Islam. The idol worshippers would throw stones at the Muslims and hurt them on the streets of Makkah.

Bilal bin Rabbah was the slave of Umayyah bin Khalaf. He was cruelly beaten by his master after he found out that Bilal became a Muslim. He would tie Bilal up and make him lie down on the burning sand and put a heavy rock on his chest. Even

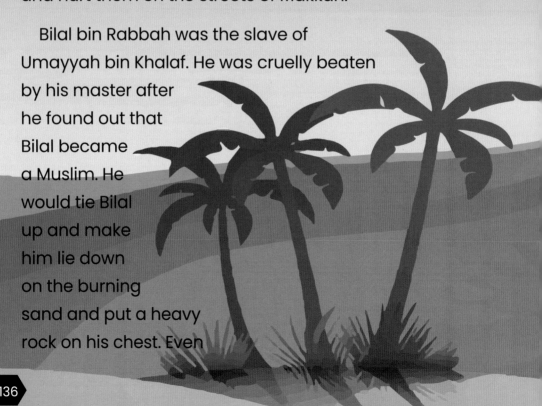

when getting this punishment, Bilal would cry: 'One God; One God.' Abu Bakr saw this, and he felt sorry for him. He bought him from his master and freed him for the sake of Allah.

`Ammar bin Yasir and his parents, Yasir and Sumayyah, were freed slaves. When the Quraysh found out that they accepted Islam, they were repeatedly tortured and hurt by them. They were tortured so much that `Ammar's father, Yasir, died from his torture and his mother, Sumayyah, was killed by Abu Jahl. They were among the first people to die for the sake of Islam. Afterwards the Prophet ﷺ would comfort `Ammar regularly and tell him that his parents are in Paradise.

The Muslims were treated extremely badly, so some of the Muslims decided to leave Makkah to find a shelter in a country called Abyssinia. Abyssinia was ruled by a good Christian king whose name was Ashamah (he was also called 'Negus' (or 'an-Najashi' in Arabic) which is his title). A group of twelve men and four women travelled to Abyssinia, and among them were `Uthman bin `Affan and his wife, Ruqayyah, the daughter of the Prophet ﷺ.

The Quraysh were very angry when they found out about this. They could not accept that some of the Muslims had escaped and were living in peace in a different country. As a result, they treated the Muslims that were remaining in Makkah even more cruelly.

The Prophet ﷺ continued calling the idol worshippers to Islam. On one occasion, while he was reciting the Qur'an, the idol worshippers were so amazed by its recitation, that they fell into prostration. The Muslims who had travelled to Abyssinia were wrongly informed that the Quraysh had accepted Islam. So, they all returned to Makkah but when they returned they found that this was not true.

So, the Muslims organised themselves quickly to return to Abyssinia. Before the idol worshippers could stop them, they left Makkah. In this second group who made their way to Abyssinia, there were 83 men and 19 women.

However, the Quraysh did not want them to escape, so they sent two of their messengers, `Amr bin al-`As and `Abd Allah bin Rabi`ah, to go to an-Najashi and speak to him. They hoped that the king would return the Muslims back to Makkah with them.

When the Muslims were asked to stand before the king, an-Najashi asked them why they came to his land. Ja`far bin Abi Talib, the Prophet's cousin, stood up and spoke to the king. He said, "O king! We didn't know anything, and we used to worship idols. We used to be dishonest, we used to eat rotten meat, we would break family ties and we treated our neighbours badly. The strong people from us would beat the weak people. We were like this until Allah sent us His Messenger from among us – a Messenger who we knew of his family and his truthfulness. He called us to the worship of the One God and stopped us from worshipping idols. He told us to be truthful, to fulfil promises, to keep family relationships and to treat our neighbours kindly. He told us not to kill and even banned us from behaving rudely. He told us not to lie or to eat the wealth of the orphans. He ordered us to worship only God alone, and not to associate partners with him. He told us to pray, to give charity and fast. We believed in him. So, we worshipped God, and we did not associate partners with Him. We believed what he said was allowed for us and we believed in what he said is banned for us. But our people went against us. They began to torture and treat us badly, so that we may turn back to the worship of idols. We left our land and we chose yours above everyone else. We hope that we are not treated unfairly by your kind excellency."

Hearing this, the Najashi said, "Do you have anything with you from Allah?" So Ja'far recited the first verses of Surah Maryam, in which it described the birth of Prophet `Isa ﷺ. When Ja`far completed the recitation, an-Najashi, his bishops and everyone who was there started to cry, with tears rolling down their cheeks.

"It seems as that these words and those that were revealed to `Isa are the rays of light which have come from the same place," an-Najashi said. He then turned to the Qurayshi messengers and said, "I will not give up these travellers. They are free to live and worship in my kingdom as they wish."

Annoyed that he had failed, `Amr bin al-`As came up with an evil plan to get the Muslims in trouble and to get them thrown out from the kingdom. He went to the king the next day and told him that the Muslims spoke badly about Prophet `Isa ﷺ. The king became angry by this and he immediately called for the Muslims to stand before him and to explain themselves.

Ja`far stood up again and said, "O king! We speak about Prophet `Isa ﷺ as we have been taught by our Prophet that he is the servant of Allah, His Messenger, His Spirit and His Word which He breathed into Maryam."

An-Najashi was happy with this reply and he said that Prophet `Isa ﷺ is not more than what Ja`far had said. "Go on your way," an-Najashi told Ja`far, "you are safe in my land. Not for a mountain of gold would I give up any one of you." He then returned his gifts to the Qurayshi messengers and told them to go away. They went back to Makkah empty handed.

Lesson 27

The Fifth Pillar: Hajj

Hajj is the fifth pillar of Islam. Every Muslim must perform the Hajj at least once in their lifetime, if they are able to do it. To perform the Hajj, you must go on a journey to Makkah. The Hajj involves visiting the Ka`bah and other holy sites and performing special actions at specific times.

The Prophet Muhammad ﷺ taught Muslims how to perform the Hajj. Many of the actions that are done in the Hajj are done to remember the life of Prophet Ibrahim ﷺ, his wife Hajar and their son Prophet Isma'il ﷺ. The Hajj is performed in the month of Dhu al-Hijjah, which is the 12th month of the Islamic lunar calendar.

Some of the actions that we perform in the Hajj and the story behind them are mentioned below:

WE PUT ON THE IHRAM

This is the special dress that is worn during the Hajj. It is made up of two white sheets. This dress was worn by many of the Prophets. When wearing the Ihram some actions that are normally allowed are not allowed.

WE RECITE THE TALBIYAH

This is a prayer which we recite when we put on the Ihram. We keep on reciting this prayer as we make our way to Makkah. The story behind the Talbiyah is that when Prophet Ibrahim ﷺ finished building the Ka`bah, he called everyone to visit it. All those who would visit the Ka`bah responded to this call and said, 'Labbayk Allaahumma labbayk' (I am here; O Allah, I am here).

WE PERFORM THE TAWAF

Walking around the Ka`bah seven times is known as Tawaf. When Prophet Ibrahim ﷺ finished with the building of the Ka`bah, he and Prophet Isma'il ﷺ walked around the Ka`bah seven times. Today, when we perform the Tawaf we walk in the footsteps of Prophet Ibrahim ﷺ and Prophet Isma'il ﷺ.

WE PERFORM THE SA`I

Running between Safa and Marwah seven times is known as Sa`i. This action was done by Lady Hajar, the mother of Prophet Isma'il ﷺ. Safa and Marwah are the names of two mountains.

The story behind this action is that when Prophet Isma'il ﷺ was still a baby, he was very thirsty. Lady Hajar put him on the ground and went to look for some water. She searched between the mountains of Safa and Marwah for water, but she did not go too far because she was scared that the baby might get hurt or attacked by a wolf. This act of running between the two mountains by Lady Hajar is remembered by Muslims when they perform the Sa`i.

WE DRINK ZAMZAM WATER

Zamzam is a special water which we drink. The story behind this is that when Lady Hajar looked for water, Prophet Isma'il ﷺ was in a lot of pain because he was thirsty, and he was crying. While he was crying, the heels of his feet were rubbing on the ground. When this happened, Allah made the water to flow from the ground where his feet touched.

Lady Hajar was delighted to see the water, but she was scared that it would flood the whole area, so she tried to stop the flowing water. She shouted, 'Maa' zam zam' (Water. Stop! Stop!) This is the reason that the special water is called Zamzam, which is still flowing today after thousands of years.

WE STAY AT `ARAFAT

The main pillar of the Hajj is to spend some time of the 9th day of Dhu al-Hijjah at a place called `Arafat. This is a place outside of Makkah and it is where Prophet Adam 🕌 met Lady Hawwa' after they came down to earth from Paradise. When we perform the Hajj, we gather at `Arafat and spend our day there worshipping Allah.

WE THROW STONES AT THE THREE PILLARS

There are three pillars which we throw stones at during the Hajj. The story behind this is that when Prophet Ibrahim عليه السلام was ordered to sacrifice his son Prophet Isma'il عليه السلام, Shaytan tried stopping Prophet Ibrahim عليه السلام from obeying Allah at the place where the three pillars are placed. Every time the Shaytan appeared, Prophet Ibrahim عليه السلام threw stones at Shaytan to cast him away. During the Hajj, we remember this by following in the footsteps of Prophet Ibrahim عليه السلام and by acting out this event.

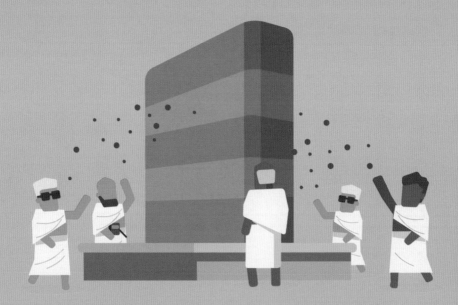

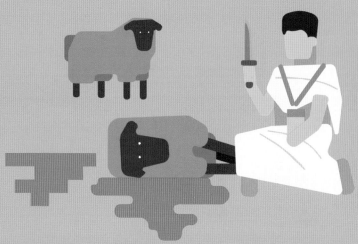

WE SACRIFICE AN ANIMAL

During the days of Hajj we sacrifice an animal. This is to remember Prophet Ibrahim ﷺ passing the test when he was ordered to sacrifice Prophet Isma'il ﷺ.

All of these actions are performed during the Hajj and they are acts to remember the events in the life of Allah's special and beloved servants.

Muslims also travel to Madinah to visit the tomb (resting place) of the Prophet Muhammad ﷺ. We can go either before or after performing the Hajj. When we visit the tomb (resting place) of Prophet Muhammad ﷺ we give our 'salam' to him and pay our respect to his two Companions Abu Bakr as-Siddiq and `Umar al-Faruq. The Prophet Muhammad ﷺ has mentioned that whoever visits his tomb will get great blessings and reward.

Lesson 28

Prophet Dawud ﷺ

The Bani Isra'il were the children of Prophet Ya`qub ﷺ. Many hundreds of years passed by and they became leaderless and divided amongst themselves. They prayed to Allah to raise for them a king who would unite them against their enemy. So, Allah chose for them a man called Talut to be their king because he was pious, strong and intelligent. But the Bani Isra'il did not accept this. "How can he rule over us, while we have a greater right than him to rule, and he does not have much wealth," they complained. So, Allah sent a sign for his kingdom.

The sign Allah sent was a wooden box, known as a 'Tabut' (the Ark of the Covenant). The box contained the personal possessions of Prophet Musa ﷺ and Prophet Harun ﷺ. It contained items which brought happiness to the Bani Isra'il. They would seek Allah's help through these items and Allah would grant them victory. In one of their battles, the Tabut was taken from them by their enemies as a punishment from Allah for their disobedience. But Allah returned this box to them when Talut became the king.

After bringing the people of Bani Isra'il together, Talut set out with his troops to fight the enemy. He told his soldiers that they will be tested by Allah with a stream. "Whoever drinks from it will not be with me," he said, "and whoever does not drink it will be with me." Despite his warning, all the soldiers drank from the river, except a small number of them. Talut took this small group of faithful soldiers with him and went to fight the enemy.

When they faced the enemy, they thought that they would be defeated. "We have no strength today to face Jalut (Goliath) and his forces," they cried. They were certain that they were going to be killed that day, but those who believed in Allah and the Last Day said, "How many times has a small army overcome a very large army by the help of Allah!"

So, they went ahead and went face to face with Jalut and his army. In the army of Talut was a young boy named Dawud ؑ, who was Allah's Prophet. He was a brave boy and when no one else was willing to face Jalut, he went to face him alone. He took a stone and threw it at Jalut's head and killed him. Seeing this, Jalut's army fell into a state of panic, and were beaten by Talut's army.

When they returned after fighting, Talut married his daughter to Prophet Dawud ﷺ and gave him half of his kingdom as a gift. When Talut died, Prophet Dawud ﷺ was made the King of the Bani Isra'il and Allah blessed him with wisdom and power.

Prophet Dawud ﷺ used to earn his own money to buy food for himself and his family. He would earn a living by making armour. Iron was made flexible for him by Allah's help, and he would make armour from it with his bare hands. He was also given a beautiful voice, and all the animals and birds would stand still to listen to him recite the Zabur (the Psalms) in a melodious tune.

Prophet Dawud ﷺ lived for 100 years. He was a wise and generous king, who ruled over the Bani Isra'il with kindness and justice. He was a grateful servant, who would spend his nights worshipping Allah and his days fasting, keeping a fast for one day and taking a break on the next.

Lesson 29

Good Behaviour – Honesty and Kindness

The sign of a Muslim is that he or she is always honest and truthful. A Muslim does not lie. Lying leads to trouble; it is sinful and takes a person away from Allah's blessings.

The Qur'an says that the curse of Allah is on those people who lie. This means that they do not get the mercy and kindness of Allah.

Lying is so bad that Allah will not even speak to those people on the Day of Judgement.

Being honest and truthful is very important. It is such a great characteristic that Allah has called the Prophet ﷺ truthful in the Holy Qur'an.

The Prophet Muhammad ﷺ told us that being honest leads to Paradise and lying leads to Hell. We must remember:

Honesty is to speak the truth.

We must always tell the truth

Lying gets you into trouble

Allah does not like those who lie

Bad people tell lies

Kindness is also an attribute of Allah because Allah is the Most Merciful, Gracious and Kind. The Qur'an also describes the Prophet ﷺ as Kind. This shows the importance and great reward of being kind, generous and gentle.

Being kind means:

- to treat people in a good way

- not to be angry at people

- to talk to people politely

- to smile at people

- to help those people who may need your help

- to share things with people who may need them more

The Prophet ﷺ never turned away anyone empty handed who had knocked on his door for food. Even if the Prophet ﷺ would be left with no food for his own family he would give away whatever he had to those people who needed it.

The Prophet ﷺ had a habit of spending everything he had on the poor before the end of every day. The Prophet ﷺ was famous for this kind behaviour to the poor and needy.

The Prophet ﷺ was even kind to those Companions who were his servants. He was never angry at them if they did anything wrong. He told us that Allah loves gentleness and kindness in everything that we do.

We must be kind to those who are younger than us, because people who are smaller or weaker than us are the ones who need to be treated kindly. It may be easy to be kind to parents and elders because they are bigger than us. The test is to see if we are kind to those who are smaller than us.

Story: Kindness of the Prophet Muhammad

Once there was a woman who lived in Madinah. She was not well, and she would walk in the streets of Madinah talking to herself. Most people paid no attention to her. They knew that she had no control over herself. Many people found it funny that she would talk to herself.

One day, as the Prophet Muhammad ﷺ was speaking to some Companions, this woman appeared. She asked the Prophet ﷺ, "O Prophet of Allah, will you do me a favour?"

The Prophet ﷺ said, "I will do whatever I can for you."

She said, "But you have to come with me."

The Prophet ﷺ asked, "Where do you want to take me?"

"I will take you to the street, and then I will tell you what I want," she replied.

The Prophet ﷺ said, "Alright, I will follow you to any street you want to take me to."

The people were surprised that the Prophet ﷺ would listen to this woman. They knew the woman did not mean what she said.

The Prophet Muhammad ﷺ followed the woman through the streets of Madinah. She was talking to herself and walking. In a small side street, the woman sat down and asked the Prophet ﷺ to sit down with her and he did.

This example of the Prophet ﷺ tells us that we should be kind to everyone especially those who are poor, weak, ill or not feeling well. We should not feel ashamed or embarrassed to help the elderly or go and play with someone who is all alone (Muslim and Abu Dawud).

Lesson 30

Sirah: `Umar Accepts Islam

When the Quraysh learnt that their efforts to bring the Muslims back from Abyssinia had failed, they increased their torture of the Muslims, and they even came up with a plan to kill the Prophet ﷺ. Among these people was the nephew of Abu Jahl, `Umar bin al-Khattab. He took his sword and decided to go and kill the Prophet ﷺ himself.

As `Umar left his house, he met Nu`aym bin `Abd Allah, who asked him where he was going. "I am going to kill Muhammad." `Umar replied. Nu`aym was a Muslim, but in secret. He thought of a way to slow `Umar down so that he could go and tell the Prophet ﷺ what `Umar wanted to do. So, he said, "`Umar, you are mistaken. Do you think Muhammad's family and relatives would let you live if you killed him? Why don't you go and deal with your family first and correct them?"

After learning that his brother-in-law Sa`id and his sister Fatimah had become Muslims, `Umar went to their house instead. When he got there, Khabbab bin Aratt was teaching them the verses of the Qur'an. `Umar heard their recitation when he came near to their house. He asked them to open the door. Sa`id rushed to hide Khabbab in a cupboard while his wife, Fatimah, hid the pages of the Qur'an in her clothes.

"What was that muttering I heard you saying?" asked `Umar. They tried to say that he heard nothing, but `Umar did not believe them. "I did hear something, and I have also heard that you two have become Muslims."

`Umar then grabbed his brother-in-law and started beating him. His sister, Fatimah, jumped in to protect her husband, and `Umar, who was full of anger, hit her so hard that she became bruised and bloodied.

"Yes, we are Muslims. We believe in Allah and His Messenger, so do what you want," cried Fatimah. Seeing his sister like this, `Umar felt sorry for hurting her. His heart now became soft, and he asked her to show him the verses of the Qur'an. Fatimah asked him to wash himself before touching and reading the verses. So, `Umar did as she said.

`Umar read the first verses of Surah Ta-Ha and was very fascinated by it. "How beautiful and honourable are these words," he said.

When Khabbab heard this, he came out of the cupboard, and said, "`Umar, I hope Allah has chosen you through the prayer of the Prophet ﷺ, because I heard him praying to Allah and saying, 'O Allah, strengthen Islam with the one you love, either Abu Jahl or `Umar.'" After hearing this, `Umar asked Khabbab to take him to see the Prophet ﷺ and Khabbab took him to the House of al-Arqam, where the Muslims were gathered.

When `Umar reached the House of al-Arqam, he knocked on the door. The Companions saw that it was `Umar with a sword by his side. They were worried that he came to attack the Prophet ﷺ, but Hamzah got rid of their fears by saying, "If his intention is good, we will give him a good welcome. If his intention is bad, then we will kill him with his own sword." The Prophet ﷺ agreed and told his Companions to open the door.

As soon as they opened the door and `Umar walked into the room, the Prophet ﷺ came forward and grabbed him by the belt and pulled him into the middle of the room. "What has brought you here?" asked the Prophet ﷺ. "O Messenger of Allah, I have come to you to believe in Allah and His Messenger and what he has brought from his Lord." Hearing this, the Companions were extremely happy, and they cried, 'Allah is the greatest!'

`Umar did not want to keep his Islam secret. He was not scared, and he wanted to go out and tell everyone that he had become a Muslim. `Umar said, "When I entered Islam that night, I thought to myself: 'Who is the fiercest enemy of Islam so that I can go to him and tell him that I have become a Muslim.'" He then went to his uncle Abu Jahl and told him that he accepted Islam. Abu Jahl was horrified by what he heard, and he replied to his nephew, "God curse you; may His curse be on what you have brought!" Abu Jahl then slammed the door in `Umar's face.

`Umar's conversion to Islam was a great boost for the Muslims. After he became a Muslim, the Muslims no longer felt afraid to worship Allah openly. They would worship at the Ka`bah without any fear or worry. This made the Quraysh feel uncomfortable about the strength of the Muslims. The Muslims now had two powerful people, Hamzah and `Umar, to protect them and to fight for their cause. The Prophet ﷺ gave the name 'al-Faruq' (the one who separates between truth and falsehood) to `Umar, because the Muslims could now invite people to Islam in public without the fear of being immediately tortured.

NOTES

NOTES